Praise for *10 Steps for Hiring Effective Teachers*

In my career as an administrator I have not seen such a thorough or comprehensive work on the hiring process. I never thought of the process as a year-round process until the author posed it that way, but it helps place the hiring procedure in a better light in course of our annual work.

This book brings to light several processes, such as Behavior-Based Interviewing (BBI), that I will definitely be including in future interviews. I will ensure participants on future interview teams read this book in order to fully understand the integrity and the importance of the interview process. This book is clear, thorough, timely and well done.

Marc Simmons, Principal
Ilwaco Middle School, Ilwaco, WA

Behavior based interviewing is the norm in the private sector, and is the best way to hire qualified people who are going to move your team in the direction you want and engage your learners in the content. This book brings that process of behavior based interviewing to the classroom, and helps you find those top people who are going to help move your department into the future.

Glenn Waddell, Math Department Chair
North Valleys High School, Reno, NV

They say hiring a teacher is a multi-million dollar decision. 10 Steps for Hiring Effective Teachers *will help you to create or refine your district's process of hiring teachers. When a multi-million dollar decision is being made you want the best process for obtaining the best teachers that you can.* 10 Steps for Hiring Effective Teachers *will put you on that path.*

L. Robert Furman, Elementary Principal
South Park School District, South Park, PA

Starting with the opening pages Mary Clement provides the reader with succinct, research-based targeted information on good hiring policy and practice. Her emphasis on behavior-based interviewing and involvement of other school stakeholders is well taken. The appendixes provide excellent tools to assist interview teams in identifying the strongest candidates. This book is a valuable tool in identifying the best teacher applicants.

Lloyd Goldsmith, Professor and Program Director

Department of Graduate Studies in Education,
Abilene Christian University, TX

Mary has intimate knowledge of the realities of the hiring process in schools and her suggestions for improvement are rooted in these facts. Dr. Clement provides practical, useful direction for school districts seeking to improve their hiring processes. This book will serve as a valuable guide for districts seeking to improve their hiring processes through the implementation of practical solutions. Dr. Clement has identified a need in the school community with this book, and she has filled the void with practical, useful solutions. The need for the book is long overdue. Mary provides sound advice about the hiring process, as well as detailed directions for improvement.

**Tim Neubert, Board President,
Illinois Association for Employment in Education**

Human Resources Administrator, Veteran School District

10 Steps for Hiring Effective Teachers

10 Steps for Hiring Effective Teachers

Effective Teachers

Mary C. Clement

CORWIN
A SAGE Company

FOR INFORMATION:

Corwin

A SAGE Company

2455 Teller Road

Thousand Oaks, California 91320

(800) 233-9936

www.corwin.com

SAGE Publications Ltd.

1 Oliver's Yard

55 City Road

London EC1Y 1SP

United Kingdom

SAGE Publications India Pvt. Ltd.

B 1/I 1 Mohan Cooperative Industrial Area

Mathura Road, New Delhi 110 044

India

SAGE Publications Asia-Pacific Pte. Ltd.

3 Church Street

#10-04 Samsung Hub

Singapore 049483

Printed in the United States of America

A catalog record of this book is available from the Library of Congress.

ISBN 978-1-4833-8018-6

This book is printed on acid-free paper.

SFI Certified Sourcing
www.sfiprogram.org
SFI-00453

Executive Editor: Arnis Burvikovs

Associate Editor: Desirée A. Bartlett

Editorial Assistant: Andrew Olson

Production Editor: Amy Schroller

Copy Editor: Ellen Howard

Typesetter: C&M Digitals (P) Ltd.

Proofreader: Jeff Bryant

Indexer: Judy Hunt

Cover Designer: Scott Van Atta

Marketing Manager: Lisa Lysne

15 16 17 18 19 10 9 8 7 6 5 4 3 2 1

Contents

List of Figures   ix

Preface   x
  How to Use This Book   xi
Publisher's Acknowledgments   xii
About the Author   xiii

Step 1–The Need for Best Practice in Hiring   1
  What Does the Teacher Job Market Look Like?   2
  Deliberate Best Practice   3

Step 2—Creating a Blueprint for Hiring   5
  A Hiring Philosophy   6
  A Calendar for the Hiring Process   6
  Emphasizing the High-Needs Subject Areas   9

Step 3—Recruiting and Advertising   10
  Where to Recruit   10
  Technology and Hiring   11
  The Job Ad   12
  Advertising Is Recruiting   14

Step 4—Determining and Training Those Who Hire   15
  The Use of Teachers in the Hiring Process   16
  Support Staff Training   19

Step 5—Candidate Applications and Paperwork   20
  What Cover Letters and Recommendations Reveal   21
  Evaluation of Resumes   23
  District Applications   24
  The Portfolio   26

Step 6—Using Behavior-Based Interviewing   29
  Prohibited Questions   33
  Evaluation of Candidates' Answers   34

Rubrics   40
One More Idea—Start With the End in Mind   44

Step 7—Planning Effective Preliminary Interviews   **45**
Job Fairs   45
Telephone and Online Preliminary Interviews   48

Step 8—On-Site Interviews   **50**
Planning for the Interviews   51
Observation of Candidates' Teaching   53
What to Learn From Candidates' Portfolios   55
Evaluation of Candidates' Personal Qualities   57

Step 9—Decisions and Negotiations   **59**
Making Data-Informed Decisions   60
Decision Announcements   61

Step 10—Reviewing the Keys for Successful Hiring   **65**
New Teacher Induction: An Important Next Step   66
Planning an Induction Program   68
An Effective Mentoring Program   70

Appendices
Appendix 1—Survey of Recent New Hires   73
Appendix 2—Checklist for the Job Advertisement   74
Appendix 3—Template for Soliciting
    Teachers for the Hiring Process   75
Appendix 4—Outline for Training
    All Involved in the Hiring Process   77
Appendix 5—Role-Plays and
    Discussion Questions for Training   78
Appendix 6—Template for Cover Letter and
    Resume Evaluation   81
Appendix 7—Prohibited Questions   82
Appendix 8—Preliminary Interview Template   83
Appendices 9 Through 18—On-Site
    Interview Questions by Grade and Subject Areas   85
Appendix 19—New Teacher Orientation
    and Induction Workshops   105
Appendix 20—Ten Steps for an Effective
    Mentoring Program   106

References   **107**

Index   **109**

List of Figures

Figure 1.1: Best Practice in Hiring   4

Figure 2.1: The Yearlong Hiring Calendar   8

Figure 3.1: Recruiting Do's and Don'ts   14

Figure 4.1: Think Outside of the Box   17

Figure 5.1: Multiple Assessments
for Selecting Interview Candidates   26

Figure 6.1: Writing BBI-Style Interview Questions   31

Figure 6.2: Traditional Versus BBI-Style Questions   33

Figure 6.3: Use of PAR and STAR to Evaluate Answers   36

Figure 6.4: Rubric for Question 1   41

Figure 6.5: Rubric for Question 2   42

Figure 6.6: Rubric for Question 3   43

Figure 10.1: Induction Is an Umbrella   68

Preface

Earlier in my career, I taught seminars for administrators on how to establish induction programs for new teachers. At the end of an all-day seminar, I asked the audience if there were any other questions or comments. An experienced principal said, "I learned a lot today about mentoring and inducting new teachers, but I realized that no one ever taught me how to hire the best new teachers. It seems to me that I need to know how to hire effective teachers before I implement a program of mentoring and induction for them." With his comments, my research on the hiring of new teachers began.

I found that the knowledge base on hiring was limited. There were some "how-to" articles in professional magazines, but research-based journal articles were somewhat scarce. As I spoke with administrators in workshops that I taught, the vast majority reported no training or coursework in how to hire while completing their leadership programs. Over and over I heard administrators say that when they had to hire someone, "we interview the way that we were interviewed." Interviews were starting with, "Tell me about yourself," and ending with, "Where do you see yourself in five to ten years?" Some principals stated that they were looking for characteristics, such as a love of children, enthusiasm, energy, or dedication.

There has to be a better way to select new teachers than relying on gut feelings. As I researched hiring, I was most impressed with behavior-based interviewing (BBI), an interview style that has been long used in the business world. Much of my writing has centered on the value of BBI in the hiring of new teachers. I have also come to believe that teachers themselves can play an important role in the hiring of their new colleagues. After all, who is better prepared to ascertain the skills of a new teacher in a given discipline than a teacher in that discipline? Teachers should know the vocabulary, the curriculum standards, and the issues of their grade and subject with intimate knowledge. Their expertise can be put to use in the hiring process, and participation in hiring can lead to stronger teacher leadership roles.

I believe that I have been asked inappropriate questions in every interview that I have ever had. All who hire must know that the only questions to be asked are those that ascertain the past experience, expertise, and training of the candidate. This book strives to share best practice in teacher hiring, with the end result of highly effective teachers being employed in classrooms where they can raise student achievement and make a difference. Having established hiring guidelines will also make the difficult job of new teacher selection an easier, more objective process.

Put simply, structured interview and hiring processes simplify the hiring process and make the work much more reliable. The more measures that an employer has to evaluate potential candidates, the stronger the chances of hiring someone who can do the job assigned. These measures include a thorough application, review of recommendations, preliminary interviews, on-site interviews, and interviews with other teachers of the same grade and/or subject. In today's world of high-stakes testing and data-driven student achievement, a candidate who can document past work with success will be a teacher who achieves success with students when hired.

How to Use This Book

This book is grounded in the current knowledge base and research on teacher hiring, while I also use examples from my experience and those of a myriad of administrators who have participated in my workshops. Although I have written it for the audience of administrators who hire teachers, it can also serve as a resource for central administration and human resources personnel. Teachers themselves can use the book for their training if they are to serve in advisory roles in the hiring process.

Arranged in chronological order, the chapters provide guidance for each step of the hiring process. The appendices provide templates for creating the forms needed for applicant reviews and interview questions. Some readers may want to begin with the appendices to see the practical applications available, and then go back and read the chapters.

Publisher's Acknowledgments

Corwin would like to thank the following individuals for their editorial insight and advice:

Dr. Marc Simmons
Principal
Ilwaco Middle School
Ilwaco, TX

Glenn Waddell
Math Department Chair
North Valleys High School
Reno, NV

L. Robert Furman
Elementary Principal
South Park School District
South Park, PA

About the Author

Mary C. Clement has been researching the hiring of new teachers for over twenty years, and she received the 2013 Star Award from the American Association for Employment in Education for her writing in the field of K–12 teacher hiring. A professor of teacher education at Berry College, north of Atlanta, Georgia, she also directs the college's Center for Teaching Excellence.

Clement's other books include *The Definitive Guide to Getting a Teaching Job, Get a Teaching Job NOW, First Time in the High School Classroom,* and *The Induction Connection.* Her articles have appeared in *Phi Delta Kappan, Principal, Principal Leadership, American School Board Journal, Clearing House,* and Kappa Delta Pi's *Record.* She has presented at ASCD (formerly the Association for Supervision and Curriculum Development), National Association of Elementary School Principals (NAESP), Phi Delta Kappa, and Kappa Delta Pi conferences, as well as internationally in China and Namibia. She was the 2012–2014 international president of Kappa Delta Pi.

Clement received her doctorate from the University of Illinois at Urbana–Champaign and taught high school Spanish and French before her career in higher education.

The Need for Best Practice in Hiring

How principals hire, assign, and provide growth opportunities for teachers likely has major ramifications regarding teacher quality.

(Donaldson, 2011, p. 27)

The value of an effective teacher can hardly be disputed. Marzano (2010) wrote, "Today it is considered common knowledge that a classroom teacher is probably the single most powerful influence on student achievement that is within the control of the educational system" (p. 213). Donaldson's research supported the claim, "There is growing evidence that, of all school resources, teachers have the largest impact on student achievement" (2011, p. 27). If, as Kersten's work indicated, "a growing body of research has confirmed the link between excellent teachers and increased student achievement," then "consequently, selecting outstanding teachers is critical" (2008, p. 355). Put succinctly, "One of the single greatest opportunities to improve educational outcomes at any school or school district is to make better hiring decisions" (Rose, English, & Finney, 2014, p. 9).

What differentiates an effective teacher from a less effective one? James Stronge's work centered on the qualities of effective teachers, summarizing research on the teacher as a person, followed by his/her management, organizational, and instructional skills (Stronge, 2002; Stronge, Tucker, & Hindman, 2004). Stronge and

Hindman (2006) furthered their work by developing a protocol for teacher selection based on the qualities exhibited by effective teachers. They stressed that when one knows the qualities, one can interview for those qualities.

Other researchers have looked at the dispositions of a successful teacher. Wasicsko (2004) developed a checklist for assessing dispositions; it included items such as attitude, believing in students, and being people-oriented. "When we hire a teacher with the right dispositions, students learn and grow, parents are happier, and district administrators can attend to the business of education" (Wasicsko, 2004, p. 40).

Once the strongest teachers are in classrooms, the issue of retention emerges. What will keep the best teachers in their positions? Put another way, why do teachers leave? Ingersoll and Smith's (2003) research on retention suggested that teachers leave both to pursue jobs that they perceive as better and because of their general dissatisfaction with teaching as a career. In some cases, less pedagogical training is an indicator of those more likely to leave teaching (Ingersoll, Merrill, & May, 2012). Could a better interview lead to the nonselection of teachers who may leave the profession quickly? Should a more thorough hiring process result in higher retention rates of teachers?

WHAT DOES THE TEACHER JOB MARKET LOOK LIKE?

The *Job Search Handbook for Educators,* published annually by the American Association for Employment in Education (AAEE), provides an overview of shortages and surpluses of teachers by field. The 2013 report indicated that no education fields are experiencing considerable shortages, but that several fields have some shortages of teachers. Those fields include "nearly all of the remedial and special education fields, the more advanced math and sciences fields, ESL/ELL, and certain Asian languages" (p. 53). As noted in past AAEE surveys, there continues to be a state of surplus of "teachers of lower grades, and for those in the arts, social sciences, English, and physical education" (AAEE, 2013, p. 53).

With reference to the oversupply of teachers in some fields, the teacher job market might be considered an employers' market, as those hiring can pick and choose from among the top elementary education candidates, and from the top art, social studies, English, and PE majors. However, an oversupply creates a unique problem for employers—having to sort through hundreds of applicants to find the right one.

Shortages still exist in certain fields and in certain regions of the country. Finding a highly qualified physics teacher for a small rural school or finding enough special education teachers for positions in a large, urban district are examples.

Faced with the challenges of filling all positions with the best people, and knowing that effective teachers make a difference in student achievement, hiring is a critical area that requires year-round attention.

DELIBERATE BEST PRACTICE

The need for best practice in hiring seems straightforward. Sawchuk (2011) reported that districts are becoming more strategic with regard to hiring teachers, emphasizing that deliberate hiring reinforces the value placed on quality teachers. Principals want teachers who get their jobs done without a lot of constant reinforcement or support, or, in plain terms, without a lot of drama. New hires should already know the latest trends, research, and best practice in their disciplines.

Despite the almost universal acceptance of the need for effective teachers, and the recognition that successful teachers should be retained, many school districts still omit hiring from descriptions of the most urgent and timely jobs of school leaders. There are constraints put on hiring and the hiring process. Time and money are always issues in hiring. Some principals indicate that excessive centralization of hiring is an obstacle in their selection of the best candidates (Donaldson, 2011). Many administrators find that teacher shortages in certain areas make hiring very difficult and that they must resort to hires who are either provisionally or nonfully certified. Some employers deal with contractual obligations, union issues, and longstanding cultural norms as constraints to hiring.

While no one can provide a crystal ball to predict that a hire will or won't be successful, and will or won't stay in the position, the use of best practice in hiring will alleviate much of the uncertainty of the process. There are indeed good and better ways to write a job description, sort candidate paperwork, manage preliminary interviews, and make decisions. The use of longer on-site interviews and multiple assessments of the candidate's experience can help to ensure an effective hire. The knowledge base of teacher selection continues to grow. I hope that this book adds to the knowledge base, while offering concrete, user-friendly ideas to all who hire.

Figure 1.1   Best Practice in Hiring

DO	DO NOT
1. Divide hiring into year-round responsibilities.	1. Delay hiring unnecessarily.
2. Use multiple assessments of teacher qualifications.	2. Use one measure or one interview.
3. Use objective criteria— experience and expertise.	3. Rely on a gut feeling or on hiring acquaintances.
4. Involve teachers in hiring colleagues.	4. Rely on non-subject-matter experts to hire.
5. Recognize that hiring is recruiting.	5. Overlook the value of making the candidate feel "wooed."
6. Know that good hiring leads to retention.	6. Think that retention of new teachers just happens.

Step 2

Creating a Blueprint for Hiring

"The teacher hiring process has always been pressure-filled."

(Tooms & Crowe, 2004, p. 50)

The often-cited phrase, "Failing to plan is planning to fail," hits the mark regarding hiring new faculty. Liu and Johnson (2006) called typical hiring practices "late, rushed, and information-poor" (p. 324). The research of Rose, English, and Finney (2014) indicated that "as many as 62 percent of teachers are hired within a month of the start date" (p. 3). To improve hiring, it must be prioritized as a year-round job, with many people involved at different levels of the process.

If you are new to a position, or striving to improve hiring, first gather whatever is written about your district's practices. Ask the appropriate people for their input regarding "institutional memory," or what has been done in the past. Consider, if time permits, a short survey to recent hires about their hiring experience. As with any survey, some of the comments and data may not be relevant, but possible trends may emerge for improvement. (See sample, Appendix 1.) New hires who indicate satisfaction with the hiring process, and who feel that they were well-informed about the position, begin their new jobs with a positive outlook.

A HIRING PHILOSOPHY

Just what is your philosophy of hiring new teachers? Does your philosophy match that of the district administration? Is there a written statement of the expectations or philosophy of hiring? Putting a philosophy or statement on paper is a good first step in hiring. Consider the following when writing this statement:

1. Is our goal to fill classrooms with highly qualified teachers to meet national and state mandates, or to do so *and* to commit to having the best teachers possible for all students?

2. How will our hiring process help us to hire diverse candidates for our faculties?

3. How can we make the entire hiring process both thorough and user-friendly?

4. How will we make our hiring based on objective criteria?

5. Will we commit to an interview process that is welcoming to candidates while still maintaining the highest selection standards?

Sample Hiring Philosophy:

Our school system commits to hiring the best, most highly qualified candidates for our students, exceeding the national and state mandates for teacher qualifications. The hiring process is thorough and user-friendly, recruiting a wide and diverse pool of candidates. Candidates will be interviewed and selected according to an established process that is welcoming and information-rich.

A CALENDAR FOR THE HIRING PROCESS

While calendars start in January, let's look at a school calendar for the steps of the hiring process (see also Clement, 2000).

September/October
- Some late hires may still be made.
- Survey new hires about their hiring experience.

- Review hiring data with human resources, central administration.
- Review the hiring budget and plan a budget for next year.
- Review any changes in state certification requirements for teachers.

November/December

- Plan and implement training in the hiring process for new principals/administrators.
- Plan training for teachers who will be involved in the hiring process.
- Solicit teacher volunteers for the hiring process.
- Work with the teachers' union/professional associations with regard to hiring practices and the use of teacher volunteers in hiring.
- Order books and resources for training.

January/ February

- Complete training for administrators who hire.
- Complete training for teachers involved in hiring.
- Complete training or review protocol with administrative staff who sort paperwork or come in contact with candidates.
- Send trained representatives to job fairs to gather resumes and complete preliminary interviews.
- Organize an on-site district job fair.
- Begin assessing the need for new hires, by school, grade, and discipline.
- Advertise for openings as needed.
- Early interviews and hirings may take place, selecting outstanding candidates.

MARCH/APRIL

- Continue assessment of numbers of new hires.
- Review current teaching assignments to determine new hire assignments (re-envisioning positions, repositioning current people before advertising).
- Advertise widely for new positions.
- Continue sending representatives to campus job fairs, multi-district fairs, or your district's fair.
- On-site, final interviews take place, with contracts issued.

May/June

- Continue on-site job interviews.
- Continue to advertise positions.
- Contracts are issued.
- Send back-to-school letters to new hires.
- Provide new hires with information about housing, welcome events, and community events.

July/August

- Continue hiring process for all job openings.
- Provide orientation for new hires; induction and mentoring programs explained.
- Contracts are still issued.
- Ask administrators and teachers involved with hiring to evaluate the hiring process and to make suggestions for improvement.
- Discuss the hiring process with human resources and central administration to further evaluate the process.

Figure 2.1   The Yearlong Hiring Calendar

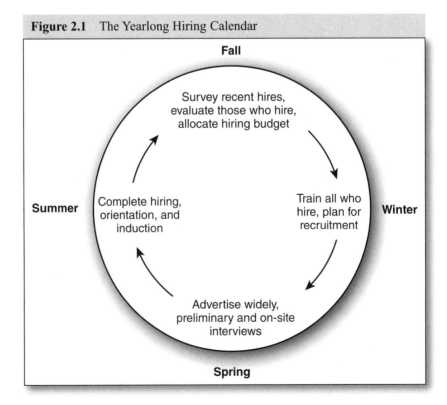

EMPHASIZING THE HIGH-NEEDS SUBJECT AREAS

Using the yearlong plan for staffing schools can alleviate issues with finding the right teachers in the high-needs subject areas of math, sciences, special education, and some foreign languages. The oldest and still one of the most effective ways to attract new teachers for these areas is to invite nearby colleges and universities to partner with the school district to accept student teachers. A student teacher who has a positive experience in a school is much easier to recruit to a position than is an outsider.

Long-term solutions may be needed to attract and keep teachers in the high-needs subject areas. Research on the staffing of rural schools is quite insightful in this area. Barley (2009) discussed programs for rural recruitment that have worked, including bringing students out to school well before student teaching for practicum experiences, and delivering online courses to practicum or student teachers so that they do not need to return to campuses for courses during this time.

Shuls and Maranto (2013) wrote that "high poverty schools most in need of talented teachers are typically those most likely to face teacher shortages" (p. 240). Their work suggests appealing to candidates' sense of altruism rather than to the more commonly used incentives of salary, benefits, or bonuses. Keeping this in mind, a school district might consider sending speakers to college campuses throughout the school year and having current teachers talk about the sense of accomplishment from working with students.

When hiring is made a priority throughout the year, personnel can be available for campus talks, working with practicum students, and building the collaborations needed to recruit new teachers to geographic areas where they are needed, as well as to subject-specific jobs. The keys listed in the next chapter apply to recruiting teachers to all schools, including those in high-poverty, rural areas, and in high-needs fields.

> I (Clement) have many friends, and former students, who have taught in impoverished schools abroad. Some accepted jobs making less than half of what they would have earned in the United States. They took the jobs because they felt that they could make a difference in Asia or Latin America. Their sense of urgency to "give back" and to represent Americans in a "good light" drove their decisions to teach abroad. If we can emulate this type of selflessness for teaching in high-needs US schools, recruiting and retaining teachers in those schools could certainly improve.

Recruiting and Advertising

"One strand of research on teacher hiring has focused on understanding how recruitment messages influence applicants' perceptions of jobs and their desirability."

(Liu & Johnson, 2006, p. 328)

"'Truth in advertising' should be the mantra of anyone writing a job advertisement for a teaching position. Then again, if all of the duties and responsibilities were listed, along with all of the challenges, would anyone apply for the job? Advertising should be the first step in what so many employers call 'finding the perfect fit.'"

(O'Donovan, 2012, p. 23)

WHERE TO RECRUIT

Because teaching is considered a "family-friendly" profession, never forget to recruit new teachers from the local pool, as many teacher education students want to live near where they call home. By accepting student teachers and practicum students from neighboring universities, your school has a built-in pool of potential new hires who know the community and the school. Administrators and teachers can be available to speak at student teacher seminars and to serve as guest speakers at campus events. A little public relations goes a long way.

Consider the paraprofessionals who are working in your school as potential candidates for jobs. Of course, these employees need to complete teacher certification programs to be eligible, but many may be able to do so and may certainly want to do so to increase their salaries and benefits.

When principals and teachers participate in state, regional, and national conferences, they are representing their schools. Use conference participation to build your district's image and to recruit other conference attendees.

Online teacher recruitment has become a standard in the hiring process. For many of today's college students, online is the only source that they may consider when job searching. "Online advertisements will net a larger pool of candidates than traditional searches to begin the hiring process" (Clement, 2006, p. 24).

TECHNOLOGY AND HIRING

The options for advertising jobs online are many and varied. Technology can also assist with gathering of data on candidates, helping to ensure a truly effective hire. Sackett (2014) suggests using technology early in the candidate review process, since technology can speed up the entire hiring process, from the job advertisement to employment. AppliTrack (http://www.aspexsolutions .com/solutions.aspx) is one example of a site that guides districts from recruitment to hiring, striving to simplify the entire process. While a district may buy programs like AppliTrack, the district still needs to keep employment information on its own website.

The district website should have a detailed description of the position, and this website should be linked to the state's clearinghouse of jobs, AppliTrack, or other commercial site used. If past experience indicates a need for large numbers of new hires, or some hard-to-fill positions, then the use of another national, for-profit site, like teachers-teachers.com can be valuable. Professional associations often maintain pages for job postings, and college career centers remain a staple when advertising jobs. The reputation of LinkedIn has grown tremendously, and it is being used widely to recruit new hires. Sites such as viewyou.com provide a video introduction to candidates in addition to traditional cover letters and resumes.

For a listing of the state websites for teacher jobs, see

www.uky.edu/Education/TEP/usajobs.html

For a list of professional associations in education, see

www.unm.edu/~jka/sts/proforg.html

www.educationoasis.com/resources/Professional_develop ment/proforg.htm

The annual conferences of professional associations should be considered for recruitment of teachers for high-needs subject areas.

National online teacher recruitment sites include the following:

www.teachers-teachers.com

www.schoolspring.com

www.topschooljobs.org

www.teachingjobs.com

www.k12jobs.com

THE JOB AD

Job advertisements should be as detailed as possible, providing information that helps candidates decide if this is a match for them. However, large districts must advertise for many teachers at a time, creating ads that state, "Accepting applications for fully certified elementary teachers, grades K–5." Even an ad such as this should be clarified:

> *Anytown District seeks fully certified elementary teachers for K–5 positions. The positions exist at seven different schools, and assignments will be made after final interviews. Candidates with experience working with at-risk or highly diverse populations should describe their experience in their cover letters, resumes, and application materials. No candidates without the state's class e, K–5 certification/ licensure will be considered. Preference may be given to those candidates with a class e and class s (special education endorsement). Only applications completed at apply-ourdistrict.org will be accepted. Follow all steps and refer to the contact information given at that site.*

Job advertisements should state cutoff dates for consideration for open positions, as well as start dates for the new employees. The ad must state how to apply, providing a link to the online job application site or the commercial site used by the district. While salaries and benefits may not always be critical to a candidate, they are very important to most. The job advertisement should have an easy link to the district's salary schedule and benefits page. How frustrating for candidates, and an employer, to reach the final stage of hiring and then have candidates say that they can't accept the position because of pay. With public school districts, this information is available and should be known to candidates before they even apply for a job. This is information-rich advertising, and it prevents wasted time and energy on everyone's part. (See Appendix 2 for a checklist for the job advertisement.)

Keys for Advertising a Job

1. Make the advertisement as complete as possible.

2. Add a cutoff date for applications and a start date for employment.

3. Provide a website location that explains how hiring works in the district. (Many new teachers do not understand that they work for a district and not a school. Explain this, as well as how final school assignments are made.)

4. Provide a link to the website page for salaries and benefits. (This saves time in the interview, too.)

5. Make a clear list of what constitutes a complete application—online application form, cover letter, resume, official transcripts, background check, letters of recommendation, and health clearance.

6. If a contact person is available to answer questions about the application process, provide e-mail address and/or phone number.

7. Inform school principals of the application process, instructing them not to circumvent the process by accepting resumes in person, and not to "promise" an interview to someone who doesn't complete the entire application process.

ADVERTISING IS RECRUITING

A well-written job advertisement provides the criteria for a checklist that will be made when sorting application materials. A job description is also a recruitment tool, as electronic links to the salary schedule, school calendar, and the city's website may entice candidates from a wider geographic range.

The job advertisement and the application process are the candidate's first introduction to your district. While today's savvy candidates are seeking jobs, their expectations for the best job can be quite high. They expect an information-rich job advertisement and user-friendly links to learn all about the district in an instant. An outdated application process or website lacking information will make a bad impression with candidates. Hiring the best candidates, and retaining them, begins with the well-prepared advertisement and what the candidates find on the website.

Appealing to the candidates' sense of altruism and their sense of service to humanity may attract more teachers who will remain in tough positions. Posting articles about the school or posting an essay by a teacher may attract a candidate. Yes, there are teachers who seek positions in the most challenging areas. For decades the US Peace Corps got volunteers for "the toughest job you'll ever love." School administrators can provide honest job descriptions and recruit candidates who will succeed in their schools.

Figure 3.1   Recruiting Do's and Don'ts

DO	DO NOT
1. Advertise in multiple ways, using online resources.	1. Rely only on ads with universities.
2. Provide detailed job ads, with truth in advertising.	2. Glorify the position to candidates.
3. Consider using teachers to recruit on college campuses.	3. Have personnel directors be the only people from the district that candidates meet.
4. Recruit from a wide pool that includes student teachers and local candidates.	4. Rely completely on finding local candidates.
5. Build a speakers' bureau from your staff to talk on nearby campuses.	5. Rely on job ads to get candidates for high-needs subject areas.
6. Attend professional conferences to recruit candidates for high-needs fields.	6. Neglect to build a budget for recruitment.

STEP 4

Determining and Training Those Who Hire

"Administrators are using different approaches for hiring teachers."

(O'Donovan, 2012, p. 23)

"Using a teacher selection model with multiple measures to assess teacher candidates is a first step to improving the hiring process."

(S. L. Camp, personal communication [e-mail], June 20, 2014)

Some student teachers think that they can apply for a job by walking into a principal's office and delivering a resume. While this may still be possible in the smallest of school districts, it would be very rare that only a principal is involved in the hiring of new teachers. The principal is a pivotal, if not the critical, player in hiring; however, many other people are involved in the process.

The district needs a written policy on the roles of all involved in the hiring process, and all need training for their specific duties. In large districts with human resources departments, the roles for directors, recruiters, and administrative assistants need to be very clear.

Professional development for all in HR should be ongoing. Questions for the district to consider are the following:

1. When applications are received by a central office, how will individual applications be directed to local schools for consideration?

2. Will the central HR office be charged with sorting applications and screening interviews before candidate paperwork goes out to principals?

3. Will the central HR office be charged with hiring a pool of new teachers, followed by assignment to individual schools?

4. If a principal is aware of a potentially strong candidate, such as a student teacher in the building, can he/she alert the central HR office of the need to review the candidate?

5. When a new building administrator is hired, he/she needs to be aware of the hiring protocol. Lawsuits can occur when anyone in the hiring process misleads a candidate.

6. When a candidate is offered a position, a clear process should be explained regarding how that offer becomes finalized (after paperwork is completed, after a board of education approval, after a background check, etc.). Having a written document, or checklist, clarifies this process.

The following chapters of this book outline the topics of training for all who hire. The topics include how to sort applications, how to craft interview questions, the need for prewritten evaluation instruments, prohibited questions, and general hiring protocol. A district may offer the initial training, providing follow-up at regularly scheduled administrative meetings.

THE USE OF TEACHERS IN THE HIRING PROCESS

Using faculty search committees in the hiring process of new professors is the norm in colleges and universities. There can be great value in adding classroom teachers to the hiring process for K–12 schools (Clement, 2013). Who better to ascertain the specific subject matter knowledge of the candidate than a teacher in that grade or discipline? "Organizations can actually use multiple interviewers as a way to increase the structure of interviews and to decrease the

Figure 4.1   Think Outside of the Box

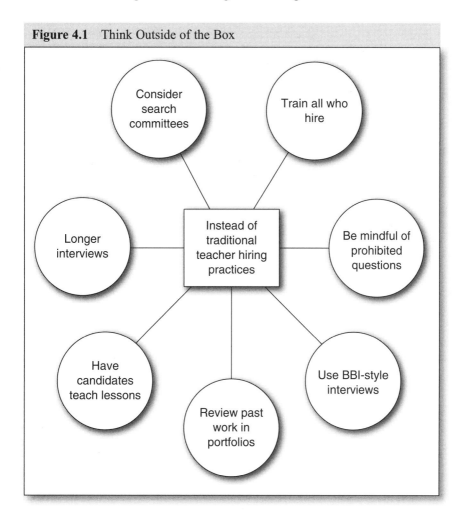

potential for bias" (Rose, English, & Finney, 2014, p. 122). The use of multiple assessments and multiple assessors of job candidates helps to ensure a strong, effective new hire.

There are many decisions to be made before teachers can be involved in the hiring process. Those decisions include the following:

1. How will the teachers be chosen to work in the hiring process?

2. Are there union/professional association issues to be resolved?

    Payment to teachers for their work?

    Seniority issues involved in choosing the teachers who will be involved?

3. What will the specific duties and responsibilities of the teachers be?

4. Who will provide the training for the teachers, and when can it be scheduled?

(See Appendix 3 for a template for soliciting teacher volunteers.)

With all of the above decisions made, the teachers will need training. The skills needed to be a second-grade teacher and the skills needed to review candidates' paperwork and interview potential new hires are very different skill sets.

Training Topics for Teachers

1. Roles and responsibilities

    Are the teachers serving in an advisory role only?

    Will teachers rate and rank candidates?

    To whom do the teachers report their recommendations?

2. Process

    What are the district's guidelines regarding hiring?

    In which steps of the process will the teachers be involved?

3. The creation of appropriate behavior-based questions

4. The creation of rubrics to evaluate candidates' answers

5. Illegal/prohibited questions that cannot be asked

6. Confidentiality issues

    What can and can't be revealed about the process?

    What happens when a new hire arrives at the school?

7. Role-plays of how to interview and how to respond to candidate questions

(See Appendices 4 and 5 for a training outline, role-play scenarios, and discussion questions.)

Are there pitfalls to the use of teachers in the hiring process? Yes, and some of the challenges may cause legal issues. A teacher involved in interviewing a candidate is just as responsible as any administrator to adhere to asking only relevant questions. A teacher who asks a discriminatory, prohibited question can open the district to a potential lawsuit from a disgruntled candidate, as can any administrator who asks an inappropriate question or exhibits inappropriate action.

While the lawsuit scenario may be rare, teachers involved in hiring must be mindful of not sharing the "inside information" that they have learned about candidates. A teacher who gossips about a new hire can certainly lower the morale of those on staff. Imagine the difficulties if a teacher says to her new colleague, "Well, you weren't our first choice, but we hope you can do the work and fit in here." Ouch, indeed.

Time is another challenge to using teachers, especially teacher committees, in the hiring process. Teachers are very busy with their regular classroom duties, and simply finding the time to work together can be difficult.

Difficulties aside, some principals have used individual teachers in the hiring process for many years. It is not uncommon to ask a foreign language teacher to interview a candidate in the language, to verify that the potential new hire actually speaks the language well. In large schools with department chairs or lead grade teachers, the expertise of those teachers is needed to identify specific teacher strengths. Besides, a department chair will work closely with the new hire and should have input on who is joining the staff.

SUPPORT STAFF TRAINING

Support staff plays an important role in representing the school to potential new employees. Their training includes good public relations, as well as the specifics of prohibited questions. Support staff must understand that small talk is not merely small talk. For example, if a candidate is waiting in an office for an interview, a secretary may not ask, "Haven't I met you at my son's day care center?" This is a prohibited question as it implies that the candidate has children, and asking such a personal question is not allowed in interviews. Support staff must adhere to the same interview guidelines as administrators, even though they are not formally involved in the interview process. It is very common for principals to ask a support staff person what he or she thought of a candidate; and, hence, they are informally involved. (See Appendix 7 for more prohibited questions.)

STEP 5

Candidate Applications and Paperwork

> *"If candidates send out letters and resumes with weak content or poor presentation, that is an indicator of their lack of attention to detail, or perhaps they skipped the classes and seminars on how to prepare the paperwork!"*
>
> (Clement, 2008, p. 21)

If one adheres to the premise that past behavior is the best predictor of future performance, then it can be implied that a candidate's application and supporting paperwork are indicators of the future materials they will create if employed. Therefore, attention must be given to sorting application paperwork for better employee selection. Each piece of paperwork provides a picture of a candidate's past experience and can be assessed. Employers need to consider as many assessments of the candidate as possible when hiring.

When the economy is rocky and jobs are scarce, school districts may receive hundreds, or even thousands, of applications for some open positions—especially those in elementary schools. Where does one begin to sort? Using support staff to do initial sorting of applications may be a way to save valuable time. Consider writing a checklist for the support staff to review applications. Each district will want to create its own criteria for the initial sorting. Considerations might include the following:

1. What constitutes a complete application? If all parts of the application are not present by an advertised deadline, then incomplete files go into the "no consideration" group.

2. Candidates should have full, current teacher certification for the position advertised. Sort out those candidates who do not have full certification (also called licensure).

3. Any candidate who does not have experience in the grade or subject level within the last three years may be eliminated.

4. Candidates who have experience in the grade or subject level in the district, or in a district with similar demographic data, may be sorted into a group for further consideration.

5. Candidates with additional endorsements to their certification/licensure may be added to the consideration group. These endorsements vary with the needs of the district but might include special education, ESOL, reading, or gifted.

While basic, the above sorting criteria can eliminate as many as 50 percent of applicants. Then, the human resources staff may review cover letters and resumes for more specific criteria.

WHAT COVER LETTERS AND RECOMMENDATIONS REVEAL

First and foremost, a candidate's application paperwork indicates his or her attention to detail. A candidate whose resume indicates that a bachelor's degree was earned in 1899 simply did not edit the resume, or have others edit it. Improper spelling, usage, and punctuation stand out on paper, and the candidate may send letters to parents with the same mistakes, causing an administrator to deal with a parent complaint.

A cover letter, either electronic or paper, should be only one page long. The first paragraph should be a professional profile that makes the candidate stand out to the reader. Examples:

Having just completed a yearlong student teaching experience in a fifth-grade classroom at Briarwood Elementary in Youngstown, I am well prepared to work in a high-needs classroom. The six additional hours of coursework I completed in special education help me to work with all students in an inclusion setting.

OR

I have been teaching seventh-grade mathematics at Connor Middle School, just one hour from your district, for the past three years. During that time, my students' math test scores have been above the eighty-fifth percentile on the state's standardized tests. As pleased as I am with their scores, I am even more pleased that my students have discovered the importance of math, and that they rush to my class to see what we are doing next.

Most support staff and administrators have time only to glance at a cover letter, so that letter should be short, concise, and attention grabbing.

The second or third paragraph of a cover letter should say something about how the candidate found out about the position, and how the candidate's application materials are being sent. The remaining paragraph should indicate that the candidate has knowledge of the district, the schools, or the area. For example:

Attached to this e-mail are my resume and the electronic application form from your website. As cited on the application, I am applying for one of the middle-grades mathematics positions, understanding that your district has three middle schools and I may be placed at any of the three if hired. My letters of recommendation are being forwarded by the career center at Roanoke State University and should arrive within seven working days of this e-mail.

I look forward to the opportunity to interview with Rake County Schools, as I grew up just an hour outside of your district, and have followed the success of both your basketball teams and bands since I was in high school. Being part of the academic faculty would truly make me a Rake Wildcat.

What about a legible signature? If a cover letter is not electronic, it should be signed. Many administrators look at the signature to see if it is legible, as a hand-written signature is indicative of that. Some district applications require candidates to write a section by hand, scanning the document into online materials. As an administrator you can decide if this is important or not. Those who want to check handwriting have probably had complaints from parents that their child's teacher cannot write legibly. It is quite a debate in the electronic age.

Many administrators say that they pay little attention to letters of recommendation because every candidate can get stellar letters from someone. Letters of recommendation can be insightful, if read thoroughly. Strong letters include vignettes, or specific stories, of outstanding work with students. A letter should indicate that the writer recommends the candidate for the job, not just for an interview. A letter that is a description of the program, and states that a candidate completed the program, is probably not a recommendation to hire at all. Letters that advise the reader to interview the candidate and decide for themselves are also not recommendations to hire. Letters of recommendation should be read seriously, and follow-up calls to the writers can add insight to the decision to interview or not.

EVALUATION OF RESUMES

When training my own student teachers about resumes, I tell them that the first half of the first page has to get the reader's attention, as that may be all that is read. A resume should be one to two pages for teachers, with clear information about certification at the top of the first page. Since everyone who submits a resume seeks a position, I tell candidates that they do not need to write this. Rather, they should put a brief professional profile at the top of the resume, followed by areas of certification/licensure, and education. Then, the rest of the resume can explain the specifics of experience and special skills.

What should the evaluator be looking for on a resume?

1. Certification/licensure matches the job opening.

2. Experience matches the job opening.

3. Experience is current.

4. The location and student demographics of the experience are similar to that of the district hiring.

5. Resume indicates past success (with students and/or in college or business).

6. If employed in the past, there was not a series of short employments. (Summer jobs that were repeated over several summers are indicative of candidate's strengths.)

7. The resume is clear, easy to read, without any spelling, usage, or grammatical errors.

What are some "red flags" to look for on a resume? A red flag is a warning, and while there is debate about some of these items, common ones include:

1. A history of short employments. A candidate who has never worked longer than one to two years in another position will probably stay only one or two years in your district.

2. A history of six or more years to earn a bachelor's degree, or attendance at three or more institutions before finally earning a degree—although this is debatable because of the high cost of college today. Some administrators believe that earning a degree in four or five years indicates persistence.

3. Unclear presentation of the resume, with errors. This might include overcapitalization of words, or a resume that is just sloppy. Some candidates create a resume and then shrink it using very small font. This is unprofessional.

(See Appendix 6 for a template to evaluate cover letters and resumes.)

DISTRICT APPLICATIONS

Some districts choose to create their own application, customizing it to fit their needs. Other districts are using commercial online providers for the application process. Some of those include:

www.teachers-teachers.com

www.schoolspring.com

www.aspexsolutions.com/default.aspx (for AppliTrack)

www.k12jobspot.com

No matter which you choose, what should the application include?

1. Educational background, with dates,

2. Complete information about certifications/licensures held,

3. Employment history (including summer and part-time jobs held),

4. Special skills, such as computer programming or languages spoken,

5. Contact information,

6. Names and contact information of references,

7. Answer to the question, "Are you eligible to work in the United States?"

8. A statement regarding the district's policy to hire a teacher and place him or her at any school in the district,

9. A statement about the required criminal background check and health requirements (or proof of completion of these), and

10. Transcripts.

Others to consider are:

1. A paragraph describing the applicant's philosophy of teaching,

2. A statement describing past success with an individual student or class, and

3. A sample of handwriting (can be scanned in to online applications).

Job applications are legal documents, and failure to provide truthful information can indeed be used to release a hire. Another use of the application is to compare the information provided to that on the resume. If information does not match, the candidate should not be considered for a preliminary interview.

Figure 5.1   Multiple Assessments For Selecting Interview Candidates

LOOK FOR	ELIMINATE WHEN
1. Clear, eye-catching materials.	1. Application is incomplete or late.
2. Letters of recommendation with specific stories.	2. Social media displays inappropriate material.
3. Recent experience with grade and subject.	3. Certification or experience is outdated.
4. Unique qualities and positive experiences.	4. Letters do not clearly recommend hiring.
5. Enthusiasm that shows in writing.	5. Letters are missing from any previous employer or student teaching supervisor.

On meeting a candidate perceived to be strong at a job fair, the recruiter suggested to the candidate that she apply immediately to the district. A month later, the district had still not received anything from the candidate. Candidates who do not understand the need for immediacy in completion of paperwork would most probably become teachers with late paperwork throughout their careers, if hired.

THE PORTFOLIO

Portfolios are an integral part of teacher preparation programs and have been for many years. Most student teachers complete a standards-based portfolio that exhibits their mastery of their college's program. This type of portfolio may be based on the INTASC (Interstate Teacher Assessment and Support Consortium) standards or standards developed by the state's department of education. Portfolios are online or in a binder.

The portfolio that a candidate brings to a job fair or to an on-site interview should NOT be this portfolio. Rather, a strong candidate should bring a small, half-inch binder with a few samples that highlight his or her work. An interview portfolio should include the following documents:

1. A sample lesson plan that was successfully taught,

2. A classroom management plan with rules, positive reinforcements, and consequences,

3. A sample of a letter sent to parents/families for communication about curriculum, classroom management, or the start of the year,

4. A rubric for assessment of an assignment, or a grading policy for a course,

5. One or two samples of student work, with all identifying names removed,

6. A sample one- to two-page unit plan or a page of a curriculum map made by the candidate, and

7. Pictures of a well-organized classroom, but not pictures of students.

As an interviewer, you do not need to ask the candidate to show you his or her portfolio. The strong candidate should use the portfolio as a visual aid when asked a question. If asked about experience with management, a strong candidate should turn to the classroom management plan in the portfolio and use it to explain how that plan was used in a classroom where he or she worked.

Some candidates now create their own websites to demonstrate their teaching abilities. They may post a video clip of their teaching, along with sample tests, lesson plans, and other documents. The candidates who do this reference the website in their cover letters and resumes. Should you go to this site? It may be worthwhile to go to such a site for the finalists.

Information From Online Social Media

When reviewing the applicants' letters, resumes, applications, and possibly online websites, you may also consider going online to find out what the candidate has posted publicly. Most employers do complete a Google search, as well as check Facebook and LinkedIn before inviting finalists for interviews. Why? Whatever you can find online about a candidate, a student or parent can also find about the newly hired teacher. Today's students and parents routinely search for information about their child's teachers, and complaints can come to the administrator's office quickly. Consider doing the search yourself early in the hiring process.

While search engines, Facebook, or other social media may not provide any relevant information about teaching, data can also be gathered with other technology. A strong online application can incorporate questions for candidates to answer. Sackett (2014) reminds readers that "the more data the better" when it comes to making the critical decisions about hiring. "Software that allows for free-form answers that help shed light on a candidate's personality, thought process, philosophy and more, are valuable" (Sackett, 2014, under "4. The Human Touch Where Needed").

Sometimes the simplest questions will help sort candidates when hundreds apply for one position. Imagine the great help it would be if online applications were sorted just for the following two items when searching for a first-grade teacher:

1. Do you hold a valid state teaching license for teaching K–2?

2. Have you taught full-time in a K, 1, or 2 classroom in the last three years?

Support staff can sort through online or paper documentation to determine these answers, but everyone's time may be better spent if the electronic program were to sort candidates initially, forwarding only those who really fit. Providing the two sorting questions above in the job advertisement should limit applications, because many times people apply for jobs and they do not meet minimal criteria.

One last value of technology in applications may be the ease of use in retrieving information. If a candidate says that he or she is qualified for a specific teaching job, explaining why in writing, that information can be easily accessed by an administrator later. Imagine the scenario of hiring someone because he or she wrote about having a personal set of laptops to bring to the classroom. This new hire promised (on the application and in the cover letter) that the laptops would be used on a daily basis in the classroom. When the new hire did not bring in the laptops, and also had no technology infused into any lessons, the administrator retrieved the cover letter and application, showed them to the employee, and said, "Why isn't this happening?" It quickly became grounds for dismissal, especially since the teacher had extremely weak teaching skills. Again, the more data, the better; and the more easily retrievable the information is, the better the whole hiring process may become.

STEP 6

Using Behavior-Based Interviewing

"Use open-ended questions that ask for specific examples of past job behavior."

(Deems, 1994, p. 25)

L ong used in the business world, behavior-based interviewing (BBI) is built on the premise that past behavior is the best predictor of future performance. In 1986, Janz, Hellervik, and Gilmore wrote about the predecessor of BBI, which was behavior description interviewing. "The behavior description interview proceeds from a structured pattern of questions designed to probe the applicant's past behavior in specific situations, selected for their relevance to critical job events" (p. 3).

In his book, *Behavior-Based Interviewing*, Terry L. Fitzwater wrote:

It has been said that the best predictor of future behavior (and success) is past successful behavior. In the employee selection process, that premise changes the focus. Now, an interview should not concentrate on what a prospective employee can do for you in the *future*, but rather on what has made that person successful in the past—and how can you best use those traits to deliver the future. (p. 3)

The BBI Approach

The BBI approach begins by determining the past experiences, skills, and training needed for a candidate to be successful in a job. Then, the interviewers should create questions that ascertain success in past experience.

In teaching, successful teachers need to have the following skills:

1. Knowledge of how students learn,

2. Knowledge of the national and state curriculum standards,

3. Subject matter content knowledge,

4. Ability to plan lessons and to do long-term planning,

5. Classroom management skills,

6. Differentiation of instruction,

7. Assessment and grading,

8. Ability to communicate with students, administrators, and parents,

9. Ability to meet the needs of all students,

10. Impact student learning, and raise student achievement.

To assess a candidate's level of attainment of these skills, a behavior-based question can be created. Questions asked in BBI style begin with stems such as:

1. Tell about a time when . . .

2. How have you . . . ?

3. Describe how you have . . .

4. Explain your experience with . . .

5. Characterize your work with . . .

6. Outline how you have . . .

7. How have you resolved an issue with . . . ?

8. How did you solve the issue of . . . ?

Each of these stems is designed to elicit the past experience or training that a candidate has had with a specific topic. These are not hypothetical questions, nor should they be. A hypothetical question elicits a hypothetical answer, and it does not provide evidence that the candidate has experienced a situation in the past. Employers should seek specific examples of past experience with all the skills needed to be successful if hired. Of course, the skills needed to be a successful second-grade teacher will be quite different from the skill set for a high school physics teacher.

Can some candidates talk about teaching and still be unable to actually teach? Possibly, but candidates who cannot explain a classroom management plan that they have used do not know how to begin to implement a management plan if hired. A candidate who can explain and show portfolio examples of lessons taught provides the employer with concrete evidence that he or she can write a lesson plan and deliver the instruction.

Figure 6.1   Writing BBI-Style Interview Questions

STARTERS	BBI-STYLE QUESTIONS
1. Tell about a time when	- how students learn
2. How have you	- subject matter content
3. Describe your approach to	- national/state curriculum standards
4. What has been your experience with	- lesson planning
5. How did you	- classroom management
6. Outline how you have	- assessment and grading
7. Characterize your work with	- communication
	- student achievement
	- differentiation of instruction

General BBI-Style Questions

Knowledge of How Students Learn

1. How have you engaged students in a lesson that you recently taught?

2. How have you motivated students to complete challenging work?

About Curriculum/Standards

1. Describe a lesson you have taught that was built on a standard. Specifically, how did you plan a lesson with that standard?

2. What are two or three curricular topics for your grade or subject that you have taught successfully?

Planning

1. Tell about your experience in planning for longer than one lesson.

2. How have you planned individual lessons? Describe a basic plan that you have used.

Classroom management

1. Describe routines and procedures that worked well in a classroom where you have taught.

2. Share a classroom management plan that you have used in your student teaching or in a past classroom where you taught.

Differentiation

1. How have you differentiated instruction to meet the needs of individual students, or a small group of students, in a classroom?

2. What are some examples of how you change instruction to reach all learners?

Assessment and Grading

1. Tell about a time when you assessed students' learning informally?

2. Outline how you have graded an individual assignment, or explain how you created a grading scale for a class. (In other words, how have you determined the grades for a certain grading period in a class?)

Communication

1. Characterize the parent communications that you have used successfully in the past.

2. Give an example of how you have sent information to parents/families in the past.

Meeting the Needs of All Students

1. Describe your experience with _____ (students in need of remediation; gifted students; students with special education needs).

2. How have you motivated students to _____ (complete homework, graduate from high school, become independent readers)?

Impact Student Learning and Raise Student Achievement

1. Provide an example of how you know that you have positively impacted student learning.

2. Share your experiences with standardized testing.

Figure 6.2   Traditional Versus BBI-Style Questions

TRADITIONAL QUESTIONS	BBI-STYLE QUESTIONS
1. Tell me about yourself.	1. Tell about the most effective teaching you have done.
2. What would you do if a student fell asleep in class?	2. How have you handled sleeping or nonattentive students?
3. What would you do if a student called you a foul name?	3. Describe your experience with a disruptive or rude student.
4. How might parents be able to help you?	4. Tell about a positive interaction you have had with parents.
5. What are your feelings about discipline?	5. Describe, or show from your portfolio, a classroom management plan that you have used.
6. Where do you see yourself in five years?	6. Tell about a past success indicative of your work ethic or commitment.

PROHIBITED QUESTIONS

When creating the specific questions for each interview, a quick review of prohibited (illegal) questions should be made. Questions may not be asked regarding nationality, race, gender, sexual preference, family, children, religion, or disabilities. These questions may not be asked in a formal interview, or in the office waiting room or over lunch or coffee, if those are included in an interview.

While this is common knowledge, the prohibited questions must not be asked as small-talk questions, either. It is just as wrong for a receptionist to ask a candidate if she has seen him or her at her child's day care or church as it is for a principal to ask about children and religion. Small talk is not small talk. If the principal asks another teacher to give a school tour, that teacher must not ask any prohibited questions as "getting to know you" questions.

If a candidate has a visible injury (cast on leg), or a noticeable pregnancy, the interviewer must not ask about those. The interviewer may ask, "Our district begins the school year on August 12th this year. Are you available for full-time work at that time?" The interviewers should ask ALL candidates this question, just as they should ask, "Are you eligible for employment in the United States?" of all candidates. This question about eligibility for employment in the United States covers the issue of citizenship or proper documentation. It is best practice to ask this of everyone, not just those who appear not to be US citizens.

It is also prohibited and illegal to ask implied questions. Asking about a piece of jewelry or a garment may imply that you are asking about marital status or ethnicity. An employer should not comment on jewelry, hair, or clothing. An employer may state the school's dress code to a candidate in an interview, and this dress code may imply that the candidate is not dressed appropriately. An employer may say, "If employed in this district, your attire today would not meet our dress code policies. Would you be willing to meet those policies on a daily basis?" If the candidate pursues the conversation by asking, "What is wrong?" the employer may then state the violation. For example, "Our dress code for teachers prohibits visible tattoos." The employer should not comment on the candidate's tattoo, but rather state the dress code as simply as possible. Do not get involved in a debate with the candidate over the issue.

(See Appendix 7 for a handout of prohibited questions.)

EVALUATION OF CANDIDATES' ANSWERS

Many administrators know exactly what they are listening for in a candidate's answer. Some use the phrase "listen fors" as they describe how they evaluate answers. They use a rubric or evaluation criteria sheet to rate responses as they hear them. What can guide an employer's assessment of candidate's answers?

PAR stands for problem, action, and result. When asked a question about a specific issue, such as student behavior, a strong candidate will describe the problem that they have encountered, demonstrating experience with that problem. Then, a strong candidate explains the action that they took to resolve the problem, and the ensuing result. For example, when asked about a common misbehavior of seventh graders, a candidate might respond:

During student teaching, I realized that having students blurt out or shout out answers was a real issue. It slowed the class discussion down, and I wasn't able to guide student learning (problem). So, my cooperating teacher suggested that I try a "think and pair" strategy for questions. I would ask a question, tell students to think quietly for 30 seconds, and then they could whisper their answer to the person next to them. After the whispering, I then asked for volunteers to share their pair's answer (action). Not only did it work well, but I could ask deeper questions because students were putting some time into preparing their answers (result).

The use of PAR as a mnemonic device to guide the listener's evaluation can be very helpful. A second mnemonic is STAR, which represents situation, task, action, and result. The listener expects to hear a candidate describe a situation, the task involved in that situation, the action taken, and the result of the action. Questions that are not about problems lend themselves to the STAR guidelines for answers.

In addition to listening, an employer needs to evaluate the answers objectively during the interview. Well before any preliminary or on-site interview, the questions for the interview should be written and an evaluation instrument determined. The same set of questions must be asked of every candidate for fairness and accountability. The use of the same questions and the same evaluation instrument creates a structured interview. "Given the time and expense of interviewing candidates, districts benefit more from using a more structured approach to interviewing because structured interviews will have higher validity for predicting teacher success" (Rose, English, & Finney, 2014, p. 108).

Figure 6.3   Use of PAR and STAR to Evaluate Answers

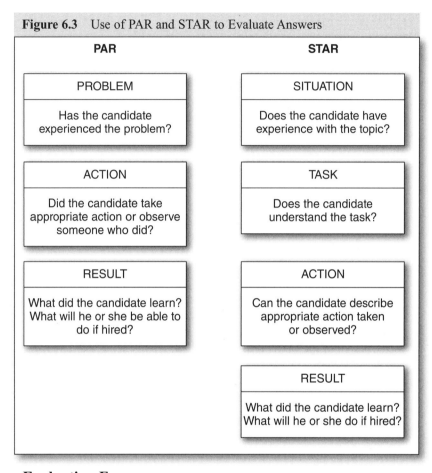

Evaluation Forms

The most basic of evaluation forms has a list of the questions and a categorical rating system or a numeric one. The use of three categories, unacceptable, acceptable, and target is common. It is easy to make a check in the category as the candidate speaks, and to then summarize how many answers are in each category. Categories may also have other names, such as developing, proficient, and mastery.

Example:

	Unacceptable	Acceptable	Target
1. Give an example of how you have linked what students were learning to their past or future learning.	_____	_____	_____

	Unacceptable	Acceptable	Target
2. How have you used student data to guide your planning?	_____	_____	_____

Many employers prefer a numerical system, so that numbers may be totaled and then candidates may be ranked in numerical order. For example:

Weak answer   1   2   3   4   5   Excellent answer

1. Describe how you have developed long-range plans. _____
2. Describe a lesson where you used technology.   _____

Learning to Evaluate Answers

For each of the following questions, two answers will be provided. Each evaluator should rate the answer using a predetermined evaluation instrument. For the purpose of training interviewers, consider first using the unacceptable, acceptable, target evaluation. Then, have interviewers rate the answers using the scale of 1 to 5, where 1 indicates a weak answer and 5 indicates an excellent answer.

Question 1: Describe your experience with long-term planning.

Candidate A: For the past two years, I worked in a school with four other second-grade teachers. We had monthly planning sessions, and made outlines of what to cover for each subject area. We focused on preparing students for the end-of-year tests by using the state standards and looking at the sample questions from the tests. The hard part was having time to work everything in for each month.

Candidate B: During student teaching, I was able to sit in on a training session on curriculum mapping, in the style of Heidi Hayes-Jacobs. I learned that curriculum maps help us to see the long-term goals, objectives, and assessments at a glance. I also liked that the teachers were building in a variety of learning experiences for all students—those who might need remediation and those who master material early. The teachers at that school will be putting maps on the school's website so that parents can see the curriculum for the semester at a glance. I would like to use maps like this to plan my semesters.

How are these questions rated? Candidate A's answer is pretty standard. He or she has done some long-term planning. The answer is acceptable. Candidate B's answer shows more much more exposure to the topic. He or she cites a theorist, which shows strong background knowledge. The answer is perhaps not a "target" answer because the candidate did not make or indicate use of a map. However, he or she sees the need to use the maps in the future. It is an acceptable answer, probably a 4 on a scale of 1 to 5.

Question 2: Tell about an individual lesson that went well and why it went well.

Candidate A (opening a portfolio to a lesson plan): My lesson about equivalent measurements for third graders went very well. My plan started with the state standard and an essential question. Then, I focused students on what "equivalent" meant and asked why we might need to measure things in more than one way. The fun part of the lesson was when we moved to our science table and the students had cups, pints, and quarts for filling gallon jars. Some teachers might find this messy, but it made the lesson very engaging. After the measuring, they completed some word problems with the same questions. I went over two word problems with them, and collected their papers to check the other three problems.

Candidate B: During my methods class, we had to write very long lesson plans with a focus, a preassessment, the steps of the lesson activity, and several assessment pieces. We also added pieces for ESOL students or inclusion students. During student teaching I learned that I had to shorten the plan because I had so many lessons to get ready. I still like to focus students by having the standard on the board, and telling them what will be on the test. I then make an outline, and I write myself notes about the answers to the math problems I will teach with. My supervisor always suggested building in an extra "something" to fill in the time if I ran out of things to do. Keeping students busy is important.

For Question 2, Candidate A's answer is much stronger. A candidate who brings a portfolio to the interview, and who uses it as a visual aid, demonstrates a teaching skill while interviewing. This candidate's use of vocabulary is very strong, and he/she uses multiple ways to teach—both hands-on and with individual practice. Most interviewers would give this a "target" rating or a 4 or 5.

Candidate B's answer is not terribly weak, so it may be acceptable to some interviewers and could earn a rating of a 3 by some.

Question 3: Characterize the parent communication that you have used successfully in the past.

Candidate A: During student teaching, I was required to create the newsletter that was posted online for parents. We also sent out some copies on paper. I used my cooperating teacher's format of including a calendar of events, like when tests were coming up, and when early dismissal days were scheduled. The most important part of the newsletter was probably the content part. We wrote about the actual curriculum, including topics, activities, and where parents could go for more information about the topics online. We sometimes included study questions. I really liked how my teacher did this, and I would continue it.

Candidate B: In the past two years at Hampton Middle, I used a website for posting announcements and study guides for the students and their families. I also sent out postcards for good news, and I made sure that each student got a postcard at home during the first nine weeks. Hampton Middle had fairly good participation at parent open houses and conferences. I have learned that the most productive parent interaction is when I show parents assignments, or provide ideas for improving their child's study habits. I have also learned to have student work available to show parents who come in for a conference. I once showed a parent her child's work and she said, "I can't read his writing." I replied, "Neither can I." This led to a discussion of how to get some help for the seventh grader in writing.

As an evaluator, what were you listening for? Both of these answers are relatively strong. Answer A is considered an acceptable answer for a student teacher who has yet to have a classroom.

Answer B is completely "target" as it evidences skills and strategies that have already been learned through experience. However, sometimes the pool of finalists never has an experienced candidate, and then an answer like Candidate A's appears to be very acceptable.

These examples indicate the need for the interviewers to discuss candidates' potential answers before any candidate is ever interviewed. Decide on what the job actually involves, and then structure the questions around those job criteria. Rating the answers becomes much easier knowing what to listen for as the candidate speaks.

RUBRICS

> *"Structured interviews are more reliable than unstructured interviews. Selection systems that are based on competencies and include structured interview questions and evaluation rubrics predict job performance with a much higher validity rate."*
>
> (S. L. Camp, personal communication [e-mail], June 20, 2014)

With the use of rubrics so widespread in education, rubrics may also be quite useful in interview question evaluations. With a rubric, specific answers are described and the interviewer has an evaluation guideline for each question. The following are examples of rubrics for three questions:

- Question 1: How have you differentiated instruction to meet the needs of individual students?
  - Unacceptable: Candidate does not use the vocabulary of differentiation and can provide no example of past experience with it. (Point values of 0–1)
  - Proficient: The candidate provides an example of challenging or supporting an individual student in the classroom. (Point values of 2–3)
  - Exemplary: The candidate provides clear, concrete examples from past teaching, discussing how to differentiate content, process, product, or learning environment to meet individual needs. (Point value of 4–5)

Figure 6.4 Rubric for Question 1

UNACCEPTABLE 1 POINT	PROFICIENT 2–3 POINTS	EXEMPLARY 4–5 POINTS
Candidate does not use the vocabulary of differentiation and can provide no example of past experience with it.	The candidate provides an example of challenging or supporting an individual student in the classroom.	The candidate provides clear, concrete examples from past teaching, discussing how to differentiate content, process, product, or learning environment to meet individual needs.
Comments:		

- Question 2: Describe how you have informally assessed students' learning.
  - Unacceptable: Candidate does not use vocabulary of formative assessment and provides no concrete example of having used it.
  - Proficient: The candidate explains formative assessment with at least one clear example from past experience.
  - Exemplary: The candidate shares more than one example of formative assessment and discusses a link between informal assessment and student achievement.

Figure 6.5   Rubric for Question 2

UNACCEPTABLE 1 POINT	PROFICIENT 2–3 POINTS	EXEMPLARY 4–5 POINTS
Candidate does not use vocabulary of formative assessment and provides no concrete example of having used it.	The candidate explains formative assessment with at least one clear example from past experience.	The candidate shares more than one example of formative assessment and discusses a link between informal assessment and student achievement.
Comments:		

- Question 3: Describe your approach to classroom management.
  - Unacceptable: Candidate does not use the vocabulary of routines, procedures, or classroom organization and rules. Candidate may describe a negative experience—unruly students, chaos, much noise, and so on.
  - Proficient: The candidate describes the use of rules, routines, and procedures and how a well-organized classroom was developed in a previous job or student teaching.
  - Exemplary: Opening a portfolio, the candidate shows a classroom management plan that was used in student teaching or a previous job. The candidate describes rules, consequences, positive feedback, as well as routines and procedures. The candidate may cite a writer or researcher whose work has been used as the basis for the management system (Harry Wong, Lee Canter, Fred Jones, or other).

Figure 6.6 Rubric for Question 3

UNACCEPTABLE 1 POINT	PROFICIENT 2–3 POINTS	EXEMPLARY 4–5 POINTS
Candidate does not use the vocabulary of routines, procedures, or classroom organization and rules. Candidate may describe a negative experience—unruly students, chaos, much noise, and so on.	The candidate describes the use of rules, routines, and procedures and how a well-organized classroom was developed in a previous job or student teaching.	Opening a portfolio, the candidate shows a classroom management plan that was used in student teaching or a previous job. The candidate describes rules, consequences, positive feedback, as well as routines and procedures. The candidate may cite a writer or researcher whose work has been used as the basis for the management system (Harry Wong, Lee Canter, Fred Jones, or other).
Comments:		

The construction of rubrics to rate the candidates' answers should allow for some variation among answers. However, the rubric provides the guideline for determining the skills, the knowledge, and the experience that the candidate brings to the job. Principals, or directors of human resources, may make a bank of questions with suggested rubrics for job interviews. The bank would include multiple questions for each area of teacher competence (lesson planning, assessment, differentiation, communication) and the interviewer would select one or two questions for each area. The use of "cut and paste" allows for the interviewer to customize each interview form with the questions needed and rubrics for evaluation.

(See Appendices 9–18 for interview evaluation questions for specific grade and subject levels.)

One More Idea—Start With the End in Mind

The phrase, "begin with the end in mind," is often used with curriculum planning, and is generally attributable to the work of Grant Wiggins and Jay McTighe. Beginning with the end in mind can certainly be useful also for planning structured interview questions. The "end" in this case is the district's teacher evaluation instrument. By looking at the evaluation instrument to be used with the new hire, the employer should be able to consider each area of the evaluation and then write an interview question that addresses that specific topic. For example, if the teacher is evaluated on student success, include interview questions that address past experience with student success. If a topic of final evaluation is attendance and punctuality, ask the candidate's former employer, college professor, or student teaching supervisor for that information.

Consider how the district's teacher evaluation is worded. Should the categories of the end-of-year evaluation be the ones on the interview template? For example, an evaluation might have categories of needs improvement, proficient, and exemplary. Do you want to make those the categories of rating candidates' answers to interview questions? The idea of beginning with the end in mind merits consideration regarding the hiring process.

It might be advantageous to have the teacher evaluation instrument in front of the interviewer during the session with candidates. The interviewer could state that the questions were designed to assess the candidate's strengths regarding the topics of the end-of-year evaluation. Providing candidates with evaluation information is also a good idea, as new hires often do not know how they will be evaluated at the end of the year. When information is provided at the beginning, and expectations are made clear, candidates are less apt to feel surprised or taken advantage of by the employer. Retention is improved when new hires feel that expectations are reasonable and that their positions are "just as advertised."

STEP 7

Planning Effective Preliminary Interviews

"Importantly, phone interviews seem to be just as effective at predicting future job performance as in-person interviews."

(Rose, English, & Finney, 2014, p. 129)

Since inviting a candidate to your school is a labor- and time-intensive event, preliminary interviews can narrow the candidate pool significantly. Job fairs on college campuses, job fairs in your district, and telephone and online interviews can yield valuable information.

JOB FAIRS

Recruiting on college campuses involves travel, but it also allows administrators and teachers to learn more about the programs at that college or university. To get the most out of campus job fairs, consider the following issues:

1. Are there fees to participate?

2. Will your district have space for semiprivate, short interviews?

3. Before committing to attend, find out how many candidates the institution is producing, and in what fields.

4. Try to meet the college dean, the director of student teaching, and faculty members. Ask them about the field experiences and special requirements of their programs.

5. Let the job fair organizer know your hiring needs so that those jobs can be posted before the fair.

6. Build a collegial relationship with the career center for future visits.

Candidates like to meet "real" teachers at job fairs. They feel more comfortable asking practicing teachers questions about the schools and students. If your district does send teachers to recruit at job fairs, their training is important. They should be aware of what to ask students, and how to represent the district. Without training, sending teachers to the job fair can be a waste of time and money.

When professional recruiters from a district's human resources department attend job fairs, there should be a clear system of how they will share the candidate information on their return to the district. This is true for teachers or administrators who attend the campus job fairs.

On-Site Job Fairs

When the job fair takes place in your district, you can determine times, space, and personnel involved. Consider the following questions:

1. How will the fair be advertised? Open job fairs may attract people with no background or certification in education. Consider a required registration and advertising for fully certified candidates in the fields where openings are anticipated.

2. Who will be providing attendees with initial information? Will there be booths for general information?

3. Will there be preliminary interviews, and if so, how will time and space be allotted? Who will interview, and how will candidates get those short interviews?

4. Will there be bus tours of the district?

5. How will teachers and all administrators be involved?

6. What will be done after the district fair to evaluate its effectiveness?

In times of economic downturn, or if a district has a wonderful reputation, a district job fair may bring thousands of candidates to the event. Be prepared for many people, including those who arrive hours in advance. Advertising that contains specific information about parking, registration, and job fair format is important. Letting job seekers know in advance that only fully certified (licensed) teachers will be considered helps to narrow the pool. If your district seeks provisionally certified personnel in certain high-needs fields, specify that.

There should be sufficient support workers to answer immediate questions and to give directions. Many districts use booths for grade- and subject-level position openings. At these booths, or tables, an administrator, a human resources representative, or a teacher greets candidates, asks one or two sorting questions, and then accepts resumes. Requests can include the following areas:

1. Tell about your best teaching experience.

2. Describe your experience teaching this grade and subject.

3. What has motivated you to enter teaching, or to apply in our district?

The initial person accepting resumes may do an instant sort of those who are invited for a longer preliminary interview in the afternoon. At some fairs, candidates wait to see if their name is posted for an interview later. At other fairs, the initial sort at the booth is used to call candidates for telephone interviews at a later time.

Some districts strive to make the most of having candidates in the district by conducting group interviews. One style of group interview is to ask a candidate to sit with a group of interviewers—perhaps someone from HR, an assistant principal, and three teachers. All ask the candidate prewritten questions, in the same order, and evaluate the candidate from their notes. (See Appendices 8–18 for sample interview questions.)

Another version of the group interview is for three candidates to be seated together and asked questions by the interviewers. This second style of interviewing can be quite intimidating, but can offer insights into the confidence level of candidates. For either type of group interview, the employers must know the parameters of what will be asked, and by whom. Training and preparation are needed. Rose, English, and Finney (2014) reviewed the research on group interviews and concluded that "if a group interview method is used to hire teachers, the link back to the job should be clear, scoring procedures should be very structured, [and] interviewers should be trained regarding their reactions" (p. 128).

The value of job fairs is that candidates meet potential employers face-to-face. The interpersonal skills of candidates are discernable very quickly. Districts can get a strong pool of candidates in just a day on a campus, or in their own district. Some districts go to campuses in late winter or early spring to advertise their district and to gather resumes. Then, later in the spring, they host their own events. Candidates who surface to the top for consideration have been met at both the campus and district fair, and they have completed all parts of the application paperwork. This sorting takes time and work, but can be well worth the effort.

TELEPHONE AND ONLINE PRELIMINARY INTERVIEWS

Skype and other online phone applications have taken telephone interviewing to a new level with video. A phone interview has always been a way to sort a pool of eight to ten candidates and narrow it to three or four to bring to a school for an on-site interview. The video dimension adds to the evaluation process by offering the chance to assess body language, dress, and overall manner of being.

Telephone interviews must be scheduled in advance, and each interviewer involved should ask the same questions of each candidate. Questions should be asked in the same order, and the interviewers should be taking notes and assessing each answer. Prohibited questions remain prohibited in a phone interview, just as in an on-site one. (See Appendix 8 for a sample preliminary interview.)

There are red flags to look for in preliminary interviews. These may include the following qualities:

1. Extreme nervousness. While some nervousness is to be expected, extreme fidgeting or inability to stay focused can certainly indicate an issue.

2. Lack of ability to express oneself clearly. College graduates who seek to be teachers should have a very strong, clear command of language. Their grammar and usage should be correct.

3. Disorganization or distraction. A candidate should take a preliminary interview seriously. Someone who acts as

though he or she doesn't have time to take the call, or who apologizes for noisy children or barking dogs, simply isn't taking the call professionally. Past behavior is the best predictor of future performance, and an unprofessional dialogue in a phone interview indicates future unprofessional issues.

4. A negative attitude. This may surface in a preliminary interview. Candidates who discuss how terribly difficult their previous teaching assignments were, or how the student teaching experience was just something to "get through" may carry that negativity with them when hired.

After preliminary interviews, the employers should summarize their notes, tally numbers assigned to the candidate's answers, and make objective decisions about which candidates should be interviewed on-site. Strong candidates exhibit enthusiasm, knowledge, and a positive work ethic in a preliminary interview. The preliminary interview is one of the multiple assessments of a candidate's abilities. It should be taken seriously by both the candidate and the interviewer.

Telephone interviews are used extensively when hiring faculty for college positions. During an interview several years ago, my search committee eliminated a candidate who told us multiple times that she was searching for an easier position than the one she had. When asked about her research and writing, she responded that she hadn't had time to research or publish due to her heavy teaching load. When asked about service to the college, her response was also that she had too heavy a load to work with students outside of class, and no time to serve on committees or sponsor a student club. She was not considered for an on-site interview because our college's teaching load was heavier than the one she described, and we expected research and service at high levels. A twenty-minute phone call can save hours of time in the long run.

On-Site Interviews

"Hire slowly and release quickly."

(Old saying about employment)

Do you remember your first on-site teaching interview? What I didn't realize about that first interview was that interviewing is a two-way street. The employer is striving to sort candidates for the best hire, and the candidates are trying to decide if this is the best job for them. On-site job interviews are stressful situations, but with planning, the stress can be reduced and objective data can be gathered to make an informed decision about who to hire.

The most important thing to remember about on-site interviews is that the only questions that can be asked are ones that ascertain the candidate's past experience, expertise, training, and knowledge of the skills needed for the job. Behavior-based interview (BBI) style questions lead to objective interviewing that provides information about past experience.

Appendices 9 through 18 have sample questions designed for grade and subject levels. These questions are starting points for the creation of a unique set of questions for each job opening. Obviously, the questions asked of potential elementary teachers will be quite different than those questions asked of candidates for high school positions.

Each interviewer must have a written set of questions prepared before the interview and must use the same questions, in the same order, with each candidate. The interviewer should take notes and evaluate while listening to answers. It certainly helps to calm the candidate's nerves to explain that you ask each candidate the same questions and that you take notes. Some employers record interviews. If this is done, the candidates must be told that it is common practice to record the interviews, and they must be told who will view the interview. The employer must obtain the verbal approval of the candidate to then continue the interview. If a candidate refuses to be recorded, that wish should not be denied. The employer may then inform the candidate that the interview will not be reviewed by all involved in hiring.

What should the employer do if the candidate asks to see the interviewers' notes or requests to know what is being written? The best answer is a straightforward, succinct response. "I am taking notes to remember your answers. Obviously, I will also be rating your responses, and no, we do not show the notes to candidates." A candidate who is overly concerned about the notes or rating, and who makes an issue of this, may well make an issue over his or her evaluations if hired. (Past behavior is the best predictor of future performance.) I tell all of my student teachers that if an employer does not have a list of questions or is not taking notes of any kind, then that employer may not be as objective as possible, may not know how to interview candidates, or may already have a candidate in mind to hire and is just going through the motions with other candidates. An employer who takes notes is one who is serious about the hiring process and genuinely interested in hiring the most qualified candidate.

PLANNING FOR THE INTERVIEWS

Communication and preplanning are keys to useful interviews. Use the following questions and procedures to guide planning:

1. Who will interview?

2. Have all been trained?

3. Who will communicate with the candidate about time, place, and details of the interview?

4. Questions must be prewritten with an evaluation template or rubric.

5. Include a template or review sheet of prohibited questions for those who interview (Appendix 7).

6. Train all support staff or teachers who meet with the candidates regarding "small talk" questions. (Remember that small talk cannot refer to any of the prohibited questions. Asking, "Haven't I seen you at my son's school?" is a prohibited question, not small talk.)

7. Review the agenda with all involved before a candidate arrives.

8. Provide the candidate with a schedule for the interview.

9. If a candidate is asked to teach a class, inform him or her of the subject content, length of time, and number of students.

Traditionally, on-site interviews have been conducted by one building administrator, and the entire interview lasted forty-five minutes to one hour. However, Dr. Sidney L. Camp, Executive Director of Human Resources Staffing in the Gwinnett County Public School District in Georgia, advocates multiple interviews with a variety of individuals and committees. "Hiring teachers using a team or committee with multiple perspectives will create a more encompassing picture of what teacher talent is needed and a more accurate evaluation of candidates with the characteristics and potential to improve student achievement" (S. L. Camp, personal communication [e-mail], June 20, 2014). Dr. Camp's district is the largest in Georgia and the ninth largest in the United States, indicating that multiple interviews are certainly "doable" in large districts.

What other options exist besides the single interview with a principal? Consider an agenda for an on-site interview that includes the following actions:

1. A forty-five-minute interview with the building-level administrator,

2. A tour of the school with another administrator or teacher,

3. An interview with a committee of other teachers (two to four),

4. An interview with the department chair or curriculum director,

5. A half hour with the human resources department to explain salary and benefits, and

6. An exit interview with the primary principal/administrator who started the interview day. This last interview may be any length of time, but certainly another thirty to forty-five minutes.

OBSERVATION OF CANDIDATES' TEACHING

The premise of behavior-based interviewing can be taken to its highest level by having teacher candidates teach lessons during their interviews. No interview question or simulation can replace having the candidate stand up in front of students and teach a lesson. Even a short lesson gives insight into the teacher's presence, persona, and communication skills with students. Content knowledge can be revealed, as well as the candidate's grammar and language usage. For establishing the context of teaching a sample lesson, consider the following points:

1. Each candidate is informed at least a week before the interview that a model lesson will be required.

2. Working with a classroom teacher, the administrator sets the time and length of the lesson, ensuring approximately the same context for each candidate.

3. The classroom teacher informs the candidate (usually via e-mail) of the content to be taught, the students' age, and their prior knowledge of the subject.

4. One option for the lesson is to send the candidate the pages of a textbook to be covered in the lesson, along with the Common Core or state standard.

5. Determine in advance who will observe and evaluate the lesson, and inform the candidate of who will be present.

6. Include basic information about the number of students in the class and the number of students with special needs or behavioral issues.

All who observe the lesson should complete an evaluation of the lesson. The teachers who observe and evaluate should have had at least minimal training in how to observe another teacher. If hiring is done when classes are no longer in session, a candidate may present a lesson to a group of teachers as if they were students at that grade/subject level. A sample evaluation follows, but teachers may want to create their own evaluation forms.

SAMPLE EVALUATION OF CANDIDATE'S LESSON, TO BE COMPLETED BY TEACHERS OR ADMINISTRATORS

Rate each item on a scale of 1 to 5, with 1 indicating "very weak," and 5 indicating "very strong."

1. The candidate had a clear voice and could be understood when teaching.

2. The candidate appeared organized and had a plan to follow.

3. The candidate interacted with students appropriately for age and subject.

4. The candidate had energy and was positive while teaching.

5. The candidate had correct content knowledge throughout the lesson.

6. Overall, the candidate presented a strong lesson.

7. I would hire this candidate. _____ Yes _____ No

Reasons to hire or not/Observations/Comments

Students are also capable of evaluating the candidate's model lesson. Students may simply evaluate on whether or not the lesson was "fun" or whether they instantly "liked" or "disliked" the candidate. However, student evaluations can provide some usable data to consider when hiring. It is important for the regular classroom teacher to prepare the students for a candidate's visit to their room, and to prepare them for the evaluation process. Not all classrooms can be used for model lessons from a candidate. If students know that their fifth-grade teacher is being released and the candidate might become the replacement, that classroom should not be used, as too much discussion would ensue about the release of their teacher. There are certainly drawbacks to having candidates teach model lessons, and scheduling those lessons can be a challenge, but watching a candidate teach may make final decisions much easier.

SAMPLE STUDENT EVALUATION OF CANDIDATE

Rate each item on a scale of 1 to 5, with 1 indicating "I disagree," and 5 indicating "I agree."

1. I could understand the teacher's voice. _____

2. I learned something from the lesson. _____

3. The teacher seemed organized. _____

4. The teacher seemed nice and/or caring. _____

5. I think this teacher would be a good teacher for next year's students. _____

Do you have any other comments about this teacher's lesson?

WHAT TO LEARN FROM CANDIDATES' PORTFOLIOS

Teacher education students prepare multiple types of portfolios throughout their coursework to earn certification/licensure. Some make portfolios for each curriculum and methods class. Other programs require a portfolio that demonstrates a candidate's mastery of program goals. The edTPA online portfolio assessment from the publisher Pearson Education, Inc., is quickly becoming a mandate in some states for certification/licensure.

A savvy candidate should bring a paper portfolio to an on-site interview. As an interviewer, you do not need to ask to see this portfolio. The candidate should use it as a visual aid. When you ask about routines and procedures in a classroom, a strong candidate opens a portfolio and shows a sample procedure used in student teaching or a past job. A student's portfolio should include a sample lesson plan, a management plan with rules, a parent letter, and a grading system or rubric for a specific assignment. A strong portfolio may show pictures of a well-organized classroom, and may include samples of student work. However, a portfolio should not include any pictures of students or any identifying names of students.

A portfolio may not necessarily make the difference in who gets hired, but candidates who bring a small binder with samples demonstrate their knowledge of visuals in teaching. When interviewing candidates, remember that they are teaching you about themselves; in doing so, you are seeing how they will communicate with and teach their future students.

Keys to Making the On-Site Interview Valuable

1. The candidate needs to know the details of how the interview will be conducted. This includes the time involved, the format of the interview, and a schedule of who will be interviewing.

2. The candidate needs to be welcomed. The candidate is deciding if he or she wants to work in this district and school. How a candidate is treated affects the new hire's enthusiasm and may affect long-term retention of strong candidates.

3. The candidate needs to feel recruited. Information should be shared about housing, benefits, and services available in the area. Candidates want to feel that if they are hired, their work will be valued. Strong candidates want to "make a difference."

4. The use of prewritten questions makes an interview more objective. Strive to quantify ratings and use those ratings as hiring decisions are made.

5. Never promise anything that can't be delivered. Teachers leave positions because their expectations are not met. Explain expectations realistically.

There may be times when a candidate "bombs" an interview. Candidates may cry from the stress of the interview, or may say "I don't know" to some of the simplest questions. Some candidates appear overly confident to the point of being aggressive or arrogant. All of these issues are certainly red flags, and they should be noted. An interviewer will know when to end an interview if needed. Be clear that the interview is over, and escort the candidate out. A candidate who cries due to the stress of the interview may certainly cry with the stress of a student misbehaving, or when confronted by a belligerent parent.

EVALUATION OF CANDIDATES' PERSONAL QUALITIES

Employers often seek to determine personal qualities of a candidate during the interview process. They are seeking to determine if the candidate is genuinely nice, will get along with other employees, and has the perseverance to do the job. Again, a BBI-style question can be asked to determine some qualities. For example, an employer may ask, "How have you interacted with colleagues in your past work or schooling? Give an example of how you were a positive person in a collegial situation." Another example might be, "Tell about a time when you faced a difficult situation with a student or students. How did you resolve that situation?"

Sometimes the candidates themselves reveal too much about their lives. If a candidate tells a long story about needing a job due to a recent divorce or the fact that a spouse lost a job, the interviewer cannot follow up with a question about the divorce or spouse. Asking about family life is prohibited, even when a candidate reveals something personal. Remember that a candidate who over-shares with the interviewer will most likely overshare with students, and this is not professional at all.

Some candidates reveal a lot about themselves without even realizing it. A woman came to a job interview in the principal's office at 10:00 a.m. with wet hair. This is a clear indicator that she didn't bother to get up early enough to get her hair dried before getting to the school. How will she appear at 7:45 a.m. on regular workdays if she couldn't get to an important interview well coifed by 10:00 a.m.? Appearance and grooming can, and should, be rated by a potential employer. After all, it is the employer who will field the complaint when a parent calls to complain about the unprofessional attire or grooming of the child's teacher.

The interview is a piece of the hiring protocol. Combined with the application paperwork and recommendations from former employers or instructors, a clear picture should be gained by the end of the interview. The use of templates to evaluate candidates and their responses makes a hiring decision much more than just "a gut feeling" about liking the candidate or not. Should employers use the age-old question, "Would I want this person teaching my child?" The answer to that question should come from objective data.

Step 9

Decisions and Negotiations

"Multiple measures including observation by trained evaluators, student surveys, and student achievement data are being used to assess teacher effectiveness in the classroom. School districts using multiple selection tools to assess teacher candidate skills and competencies during the hiring process are more likely to hire effective teachers."

(S. L. Camp, personal communication [e-mail], June 20, 2014)

G athering objective data about candidates may not guarantee a strong hire, but it certainly improves the chances of employing a strong new teacher. How does one go about making those final decisions?

The district should have a policy about the decision-making process, and, more importantly, should follow their own blueprint! The policy should not be a secret. It should be published and accessible for those involved in hiring. What does such a policy look like? Policies vary based on each district, and may include teacher union requirements. Guidelines for the development of a district policy include the following questions:

1. Who makes the final recommendation? (building-level principal? human resource director? superintendent?)

2. Once a final recommendation is made, how is the candidate "cleared" for all of the district employment requirements? These include criminal background check, health form filed, insurance form completed, and so on.

3. When does the candidate receive final approval from the hiring entity? This is often a board of education vote.

4. How are contracts delivered, and what is the time line for receipt of a signed contract?

5. How is the candidate informed of final decisions, and how is the candidate updated regarding orientation and first day of work?

6. How are other faculty members informed of the decisions regarding new hires, and how much information about new hires is given to the building faculty?

7. How is the newly hired faculty member updated regarding the district's induction and mentoring program?

Making Data-Informed Decisions

Employers who use evaluation forms for interviews often ask, "What do I do if the numbers for a candidate are high, but I am still thinking that a second candidate is better?" There may be different reasons for this. Perhaps the evaluator didn't ask the right questions, or was impressed with the charisma of a certain candidate. Everyone has biases, and some employers seek to hire candidates who exhibit a background and experience similar to their own. Some interviewers want to consider a sympathy factor, or the factor of how badly someone needs a job. There are some administrators who insist on hiring someone that they know, or someone known by an acquaintance. Others do not like to hire exceptionally talented people because they fear that the person will outshine them. This type of hiring is not data-informed, and it can cause issues when the new hire arrives for work in the building.

When a new hire is chosen for reasons other than true merit, he or she may not be able to do the job. Veteran teachers lose faith in an administrator, and a district, when this happens. Morale drops. Most importantly, what happens to student achievement?

When making final decisions, consider the candidate's experience as a predictor of future performance. A candidate who is positive and confident in an interview should be positive and confident in front of students and when communicating with parents. A candidate who can explain, and show, a rubric used to grade students' essays, knows how to create rubrics and is much more apt to use them than a candidate who says, "I'm not sure what you mean by rubric." Asking subject matter–specific questions should ascertain if the candidate has the appropriate background in content.

To reiterate, use premade evaluation forms to assess the candidates' paperwork and their preliminary and final interviews. Refer to letters of recommendation and follow-up calls made to former employers and professors. Then, use the data gathered to formulate a final decision.

When multiple people are involved in providing recommendations, there may be disagreement. This is natural, and it can be healthy. Generally, though, disagreement can be an indicator that the candidate does not appear strong to all who have been interviewers. Disagreement is lessened when all who interview have a clear picture of the criteria needed for an effective new hire. The training of those who hire is essential.

DECISION ANNOUNCEMENTS

When final decisions are made, how those announcements are made to the existing faculty can be important in the acceptance of the new hire. Consider having a template of what is announced—including only name, start date of employment, and position. "Please welcome Sam Rodriguez to our faculty. He will begin teaching on August 3rd at Pleasant High School in the English department."

It is NOT recommended that you announce any other background about employees. It is not the job of the employer to reveal family status or college or university or any personal information. If the school publishes information about a new hire in a school newsletter or in the local paper, this information should come directly from the employee, with his or her express permission.

Some administrators introduce new faculty in orientation meetings with glowing statements about them. "We are so pleased that Angela Baxter has joined our faculty. A graduate of Radcliffe, she earned her teacher certification from Memphis State and wrote her master's thesis about at-risk youth. What an honor for us that she chose to work here, moving her family to our city and enrolling her children in our elementary school." This is too much information. While the administrator is well-meaning, other teachers are already unhappy that the "boss" is saying glowing things about someone who hasn't proven herself. Employee morale is a fragile thing, and while welcoming a new teacher is important, revealing too much about a new employee is not helpful.

Stories still abound about three hundred candidates applying for one elementary school position. When one candidate is finally selected from such a pool, care needs to be taken about that new hire's welcome and induction into the faculty. Tremendous pressure is placed on a new teacher who finds out that there were three hundred other candidates. If he or she makes one mistake, or even has a bad day, other teachers may talk about why a more effective candidate wasn't hired. Of course, with so many candidates, all teachers will never be satisfied with the new hire. An administrator should be truly supportive of all new hires, and be empathetic toward the stress of a new hire in a building where hundreds of people wanted a job.

With regard to the high-needs fields, there are school districts that resort to hiring personnel who are not fully certified. If a hire is someone with a provisional certification and/or is working on licensure while teaching, special support has to be provided to the new hire. Generally, there are state guidelines for the mentoring and supervision of a provisionally certified teacher. It is not realistic to expect teachers down the hall to provide all of the help that the new teacher will need. Veteran teachers can be quite resentful of new hires who have not completed teacher certification programs. They do not have the time, or training, to serve as a teacher educator to that new hire. When hiring a provisionally certified person, a paid mentor and a supervisor have to be employed to teach and guide the new person. The new hire may need to miss some time in order to complete college requirements. While it is sometimes necessary to hire teachers who have not completed teacher education programs, having the yearlong recruitment and hiring plan will alleviate some of the last-minute hiring issues and the issue of finding teachers in high-needs fields.

Notification of Nonhires

When final decisions are made, and a winning candidate accepts a job, how are the nonhires notified? E-mail is considered too impersonal by many for this type of notification. Phone calls are generally made to nonhires. Consider an outline of what to say, keeping the conversation very professional and succinct.

1. Introduce yourself, verifying with whom you are talking.

2. State that the position has been filled.

3. Thank the candidate for his or her time and interest in your district.

4. Do not divulge why that candidate was not hired.

5. Do not reveal who was hired or why.

6. Graciously, yet assertively if necessary, terminate the phone conversation.

7. Document the time and date of the call and any unusual questions or comments made by the candidate.

Legal Issues

When a search ends and a candidate is hired, follow the district's policies about storage of paperwork from the hiring process. This will vary from district to district.

Some candidates ask why they were not hired, or what recommendations the employer may have regarding areas of improvement for a future interview. It is best not to answer either question. An employer may state that that information is not shared with candidates. Some candidates try to find out a reason, no matter what is said. They may call someone they know in the district, or call a support staff person they met in the interview. Prepare all who hire not to reveal reasons behind hiring decisions.

Consider the following scenarios for discussion:

1. Some colleges and universities have better reputations for their teacher education programs than others. How much weight do you give to the institution from which the candidate earned his or her degree? Should this be a consideration at all?

2. If a committee makes a recommendation for a new hire to an administrator, and the administrator chooses a different candidate for the position, what are the ramifications of this action? Should the administrator discuss the decision with the committee, after his or her decision is made?

3. Generally, a building-level administrator makes a recommendation, and it is forwarded to central administration. If that recommendation is reversed, what steps should the building administrator take to find out reasons for the decision?

4. In your district, has a board of education ever not hired a recommended candidate? If so, why? How can this situation be avoided in the future?

5. When a new hire is made, gossip about the process or about the person can ensue. How can administrators stop rumors and/or unnecessary discussions among faculty?

6. Discuss this statement: When there is an absence of information, people create their own stories. How can you keep people informed about ongoing hiring without revealing private information?

Step 10

Reviewing the Keys for Successful Hiring

Those involved in hiring have probably heard some clichés about the hiring process. "Hire slowly—release quickly." "When in doubt, go with your gut." "Your first reaction is probably the right one." "A really needy candidate will probably give more to the position." "Don't look at grades, they don't mean a lot." "Better to hire the devil that you know than the one you don't." "Don't hire the candidate with the master's degree. They think they know too much and they cost more."

The stakes are too high in today's schools to rely on folk wisdom or old sayings for the hiring of new teachers. A new hire must be able to walk into a classroom and assume all of the duties of a veteran teacher on the first day. When a teacher does not perform well, the administrator's workload increases, as he or she must intervene and attempt to improve the teacher's instruction. If remediation does not work, the administrator must spend an inordinate amount of time releasing the employee.

To summarize the theme of this book, there are several keys to remember:

1. Past behavior is the best predictor of future performance.

2. An information-rich job advertisement should be as specific as possible with regard to the qualifications and duties of a candidate.

3. Sorting candidates' paperwork is important, and it should be done with prewritten evaluation guidelines.

4. Base all decisions on objective data gathered from evaluations of a candidate's paperwork and the preliminary and final interviews.

5. Ask only interview questions that relate to the candidate's training, experience, and expertise to do the job advertised.

6. Asking hypothetical questions yields only hypothetical answers. Employers should ask what candidates have done in the past, to ascertain the knowledge and skills that they have in their repertoire.

7. Have a reason for every interview question asked. Each interview question should lend itself to evaluation.

8. Train all employees who are involved in the hiring process.

9. Share prohibited questions with all who interview and with support staff who meet with candidates.

10. Use teachers to interview for subject matter and grade-level expertise, but provide training before teachers serve on search or interview committees.

11. Keep good records of phone calls and/or e-mails to finalists.

12. Use the district's guidelines for making final decisions and for informing current faculty about new hires.

13. Welcome new hires, but do not overshare information about them.

14. Provide induction for all new hires. Orientation is part of induction, but ongoing, continuing professional development and mentoring are needed.

15. Always be aware of district policies and legal issues when hiring and providing orientation to new hires.

NEW TEACHER INDUCTION: AN IMPORTANT NEXT STEP

"If you have a strong selection process in place that rigorously assesses your candidates on multiple measures, you should have a good sense of where your new hires are strong and weak. You can use that information

to set development goals and benchmarks for your new hires beginning on day one."

(S. L. Camp, personal communication
[e-mail], June 20, 2014)

The retention of strong employees begins with a positive hiring experience, followed by planned orientation and induction. Most districts try to provide all the information to new hires in a one-day program the day before preplanning or the arrival of students. Worse yet, new hires may be taken out of preplanning time in their classrooms for orientation. An ideal situation is to schedule new teacher orientation for at least two days and to pay teachers an honorarium for attending. Then, teachers will attend preplanning with all other faculty and have time to work in their classrooms to prepare for student attendance.

What should be included in orientation? The first rule is to be welcoming. Provide soft drinks, coffee, and snacks, including healthy ones. Those who direct orientation should consider the time as teachable moments, and they should not simply read handouts to the participants. For introductions, have new hires introduce themselves to the group as they will introduce themselves to their own students on the first day of school. Consider having new hires work in pairs to answer questions and to work in small groups to role-play scenarios. Allow ample time for participants' questions. (See Appendix 19 for steps.)

Orientation should include the following topics:

1. Attendance.

2. An overview of administrators and directors and where to go for specific issues. Include the director of special education, instructional coaches, discipline administrator, and director of counseling.

3. An overview of the district and building classroom management and discipline policies. Don't just lecture to new hires. Provide paper and markers for them to make a classroom management poster with other teachers in their grade level during a session of the orientation. This activity is hands-on, and the teachers leave feeling that time was well spent.

4. Do not try to teach every policy during the two-day orientation. Allow time to explain the ongoing seminars for new hires and the mentoring program. Explain that these future sessions

are planned based on the school year, and that each topic will be addressed in a timely manner at these monthly sessions.

5. Have new hires work with their mentors in their classrooms as a part of orientation.

For more orientation and induction ideas, see, for example, Clement and Wilkins, (2011).

PLANNING AN INDUCTION PROGRAM

Figure 10.1   Induction Is an Umbrella

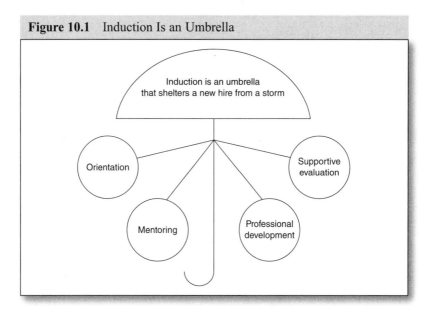

To many teachers, the first year of teaching feels like being hit by a tsunami, or at least a heavy rainstorm. Induction is an umbrella that shelters the new hire from the storms of the first year of teaching. At its best, induction should be a five-year process, or at least a two-year one. Induction includes orientation, planned and ongoing seminars throughout the first years, and mentoring. Additionally, evaluation of new hires should be supportive in nature. Many models exist for starting or improving induction programs. By surveying teachers in their second and third years of teaching, an administrator can gather data on the specific needs of the programs for new hires. A key for a successful induction program is to have one person who serves as the coordinator of the program. This person must be knowledgeable about the district, interested in teaching the professional development seminars for new hires, trained for the position, and above all, sympathetic to the needs of new teachers.

By spreading the induction seminars throughout the year, teachers have time to absorb the material presented. Teachers should find their induction seminars to be a type of support group, where there is safety in asking questions. Consider planning the seminars based on the school calendar.

> Fall topics: communication with parents, expectations for parent night, more with classroom management and discipline, and grading issues.

> Winter: student achievement, special education help, and differentiation.

> Spring: all about testing, time and stress management, student motivation, and finishing the school year.

When planning monthly meetings, guest speakers may be other teachers in the district. Teachers like sharing with other teachers, and the cost of bringing in outsiders can be prohibitively expensive. If a guest speaks, there should still be time for the teachers to share their own issues with just the program coordinator. This builds the camaraderie to ease the feelings of isolation so often felt by new teachers.

Successful induction programming includes these other keys:

1. Work with the teachers' association or union when planning induction activities. Work out details such as release time for the seminars, since some unions mandate how much extra time a teacher can be expected to be in meetings.

2. These seminars should be nonevaluative ones. This means that if a teacher shares a difficult day or experience, the experience will not be used as a black mark on his or her record. Stress confidentiality, and review with teachers how they are evaluated as a separate matter.

3. Always celebrate successes. Start sessions with, "What is the best thing that has happened in your classroom since we last met?" or a similar positive icebreaker activity.

4. Provide snacks and a comfortable environment.

5. When there are a large number of new hires in a district, consider dividing the teachers into grade-level and subject matter groups. High school teachers face very different challenges than their peers in a kindergarten classroom, and having separate induction seminars for the different levels is very helpful. Even within the groups, consider small group activities for the different grade and subject levels. Sometimes just talking to one other teacher of the same grade or subject is the highlight of a seminar for a participant.

AN EFFECTIVE MENTORING PROGRAM

Mentoring is one piece of a complete induction program. The pairing of a more experienced teacher with a new hire provides that new teacher with a confidante, a role model, and someone to turn to with questions and concerns. Simply assigning a teacher to be a mentor does not make mentoring work. Just as with the overall induction program, a mentor program must be planned; it must have a coordinator, and mentors must have the appropriate training. (See Appendix 20.)

When starting or updating the mentoring program, consider who will mentor the new teachers. A strong mentor may have the following characteristics:

1. Knows how to implement instruction that works,

2. Understands how to raise student achievement,

3. Can share his or her knowledge of teaching strategies and classroom management,

4. Is accepting of the new teacher's ideas and struggles,

5. Respects issues of confidentiality,

6. Can advise the new teacher regarding parent communication and involvement,

7. Can suggest time and stress management strategies, and

8. Models professionalism.

Mentors need training in their roles and responsibilities, including the timetable for working with their assigned new teachers. Will the district provide some shared planning time or will the mentor/new teacher pairings need to meet on their own time? Will mentors be volunteers or compensated for their work? Other topics to be covered in mentor training include the following:

1. How to mentor/teach another adult. (Teaching fifth grade and helping a new fifth-grade teacher are two separate skill sets.)

2. How to observe in another teacher's classroom and give useful feedback. (Determine if observing in the teacher's classroom is part of the mentoring program or not. Observations can be very useful.)

3. Interpersonal communication skills.

4. Updates on the hot topics of the district for the year (new testing, new textbook series, etc.).

5. When to report a new teacher's issues to someone else in the district, and when the information should remain confidential.

The final step in making mentoring and other induction programs successful is evaluation of the programs offered. New teachers should have the opportunity to evaluate their orientation sessions, their ongoing induction seminars, and their mentoring program. The new teachers should evaluate the mentor, rating that person's helpfulness, availability, knowledge, and collegiality. "How does one demonstrate the effectiveness of induction programs? First, one can look at the retention of new teachers. . . . In this age of accountability, one may research areas of student achievement" (Clement & Wilkins, 2011, p. 25). Evaluation of the induction program provides administrators and teachers with many opportunities for action research; but, more importantly, even quick surveys provide much needed information for the improvement of the programs. While retention begins with hiring, the induction and support of the new hires can ensure higher retention rates of effective teachers.

Evaluation of the teachers must be done to ensure that effective teachers are doing their jobs. However, even teacher evaluation can be supportive in nature, not just an administrator pointing out every mistake made to the new hire. Truly supportive administrators provide supportive evaluation that helps the new hire to grow professionally, keeping in mind the developmental readiness of each hire.

Appendices

APPENDIX 1

Survey of Recent New Hires

As our district strives continually to improve its hiring practice, we ask you to complete the following survey about your hiring experience in our school system.

For each of the following, indicate your agreement or disagreement with the statement. A 1 indicates complete disagreement, and a 5 indicates complete agreement.

   Disagree 1————2————3————4————5 Agree

1. The job advertisement provided clear, correct information. _____

2. The application process was clear and user-friendly.   _____

3. I gained valuable information about the position
   in the preliminary and/or on-site interviews.   _____

4. Everyone I met during the hiring process
   was courteous and welcoming.   _____

5. The time frame between application and hearing
   about an interview was appropriate.   _____

6. The time frame between the final interview and
   the offer was appropriate.   _____

7. I felt that I was recruited throughout the hiring
   process and that my skills were valued.   _____

8. Now that I am in my new job, I feel that the
   expectations of the position were clearly explained
   in the hiring process.   _____

What suggestions do you have for the improvement of our school system's hiring process?

APPENDIX 2

Checklist for the Job Advertisement

1. _____ Decide on where to advertise: district website, Appli-Track or other for-profit site, state teacher job site, local newspaper, and within the district as mandated by some teacher unions.

2. _____ List all application materials needed: cover letter, resume, letters of recommendation, list of current references, proof of certification.

3. _____ List all required criteria for the job: specific certification and endorsements, experience with students of similar demographic backgrounds to those in the district, willingness to move from grade level to grade level. Listing additional considerations, such as "preference given to candidates with six hours of special education coursework" may be added.

4. _____ Provide easily accessible information about salary and benefits.

5. _____ Be specific about whom to contact if there are questions. If no one will answer questions or e-mails, state that in the ad. Example: Applicants should adhere to the steps in this advertisement for submitting all information. No further questions about the position can be answered at this time.

6. _____ Consider a line about "walk-in applications," if those are not desired. Example: Applications that are brought to a principal will not be considered. Please follow the steps outlined in this position description.

7. _____ If there are deadlines for application and for a start date for the position, list those.

8. _____ Describe the district, its community, and other positives about the area.

APPENDIX 3

Template for Soliciting Teachers for the Hiring Process

Name:

Areas of grade and subject matter expertise:

Total years of classroom teaching experience:

Years in our school/district:

1. List previous experience with hiring, interviewing, or search committee work. (This may include work in fields outside of education.)

2. List any training you have had with regard to hiring or interviewing.

3. List other committees on which you have served in your school or district.

4. Why are you interested in reviewing candidate applications or interviewing candidates?

I understand that this work is voluntary and that I will not receive monetary payment. _____yes

I understand that I will need to complete training to participate in the hiring process. _____ yes

I understand that I will need to adhere to strict confidentiality measures if I participate in hiring procedures. _____ yes

APPENDIX **4**

Outline for Training All Involved in the Hiring Process

1. _____ Determine who needs training and who will provide training. (Consider training teacher volunteers and support staff.)

2. _____ Share the district's hiring philosophy.

3. _____ What are each participant's roles and responsibilities?

4. _____ Describe the time line for hiring; include how many new hires are needed and the grade and subject areas needed.

5. _____ Show a job advertisement. Explain the complete application and interview process. (Many teacher share misinformation with candidates, leading to difficult situations and potential legal issues.)

6. _____ Explain behavior-based interviewing and how it will be used in preliminary and on-site interviews.

7. _____ Explain the issues of prohibited questions in interviews.

8. _____ Share the decision-making process for hiring after interviews. Who is involved, and what is that time line?

9. _____ Use time in training to have teachers, administrators, and other participants complete the role-play scenarios from this book.

10. _____ Answer other questions about the hiring process.

11. _____ Inform participants about the orientation and induction programs for new hires. Ask for volunteers to participate in the induction of new teachers or to serve as mentors.

12. _____ Have all participants complete an evaluation form of their training.

APPENDIX 5

Role-Plays and Discussion Questions for Training

1. A member of the teacher interview team has just asked the candidate to describe how she has communicated with parents in her past teaching experience. The candidate answers by saying, "I am the parent of two children, so I know the information that I want from my children's teachers. I want to know . . ." With regard to the disclosure about her own children, can the interview committee ask a follow-up question about the family? What can the committee ask as a follow-up question to the candidate?

Answers: NO. Even when a candidate reveals information about family, the committee cannot follow up with personal questions.

The committee might follow up with a question requesting a specific example about parent newsletters, phone calls, or conferences.

2. Role-play a scenario where a candidate talks entirely too long about a question. Specifically, how would you, as an interviewer, diplomatically guide the candidate to quit talking?

3. You have asked a candidate to describe how he has worked to keep students actively engaged in difficult work. To your surprise, the candidate begins to cry. What is your reaction? What will you say and do at this point? How does this behavior affect your overall assessment of the candidate?

4. You have asked the candidate about her knowledge and interest in your school district. The candidate answers by explaining, in vivid detail, her recent surgery. What is your response to this explanation? If the surgery description is particularly embarrassing, does this influence your judgment of the candidate? What if the candidate's answer to this same question is a long description of her recent divorce as a need for a job in your district?

5. You have interviewed three people as finalists for a position. Two of the three have stellar credentials, communication skills, and experience. It is truly a toss-up between the two. How will you make the final decision? What might the discussion of a committee or of a principal and another building administrator sound like as this decision is made? (Role-play the discussion.) What about considering the life circumstances of the candidates? What if, even though you couldn't ask about it, you know that one candidate desperately needs the job due to family issues, while the other is married to professional with an income?

6. A candidate arrives at your school at 9:00 a.m. in jeans and a T-shirt and begins walking around the hallways, peeking into classrooms. He has an interview scheduled for 2:00 p.m. with you. A teacher reports that a stranger is in the hallways. Role-play the conversation with this candidate. (Hint: Perhaps the candidate says something like, "I wanted to get to know the school before our interview. I will go home and change before our two o'clock appointment.") Will you interview him later?

7. A candidate has just interviewed with you, and her answers were stellar. She knows all of the vocabulary of teaching and is articulate about hot topics in education. However, in a follow-up phone call to one of her references, the department chair does not speak highly of the candidate. The department chair speaks of the assignment given the teacher and of how many semesters the candidate taught there. Role-play your conversation with the department chair about the candidate. How does this conversation influence your decision?

8. A candidate comes to your school for an interview at 10:00 a.m. and has wet hair. His career clothes are appropriate. Should the wet hair affect your consideration of the candidate?

9. A candidate with excellent letters of recommendation and two years of experience is interviewing with you. She speaks with informal, colloquial language, including grammatical mistakes. How does the candidate's language affect your decision to hire? What if the candidate's language mirrors that of the community in which the school is located? (Consider, perhaps, the use of "y'all" or other regional dialects in certain parts of the country.)

10. A candidate for a position working with preK, kindergarten, or first grade arrives for an interview wearing denim pants, a bright T-shirt, and a colorful vest. He shares that this is normal dress for school, as teachers of young children need to be ready for paint spills, milk stains, and reading time on the rug. What is your reaction to the candidate's attire?

11. Many candidates do overshare. What is your reaction to a teacher who states her marital or family status early in the interview? (This might include stating her relationship with a gay partner.)

12. You have asked a question regarding the candidate's interest and knowledge in your district or school. He smiles and replies, "I am interested because you have a job opening." What is your reaction to this answer?

APPENDIX **6**

Template for Cover Letter and Resume Evaluation

For each of the following, rate the item based on a scale of 1 to 5, with 5 being the highest score.

Very poor/unacceptable 1——2——3——4———5 Excellent quality

1. Cover letter is well written and states qualifications.   _____

2. Cover letter is free of grammatical, spelling, and usage errors.   _____

3. Candidate states at least one success with students or candidate's own education.   _____

Resume

4. Resume is easy to read, clearly written.   _____

5. Resume is free of grammatical, spelling, and usage errors.   _____

6. Certification/licensure match job advertisement.   _____

7. Experience matches job opening.   _____

8. Resume highlights accomplishments with students or in previous job or college program.   _____

9. No gaps in education or work experience.   _____

10. Resume captured the reader's attention for a positive reason.   _____

Other sorting criteria to personalize the template: (experience with diverse populations, etc.)

APPENDIX **7**

Prohibited Questions

(This sheet may be distributed and placed on tables when committees interview.)

- You may not ask questions about the following topics:
  - Nationality
  - Race
  - Gender
  - Sexual preference
  - Family
  - Children
  - Religion
  - Disabilities
- Questions may not be asked as small talk. You may not say:
  - "What a pretty ring. Tell me about it."
  - "What a unique scarf. Does the pattern mean something?"
  - "You look so familiar. Where have we met? Perhaps at my daughter's school?"
- You may not comment on a visible injury, pregnancy, use of a cane, wheelchair, or other physical issue.

What can be asked if the candidate discloses family or other personal information?

- It is still prohibited to ask a follow-up question about that personal information.
  - Example: Candidate states, "I am job searching in your district because my husband's job brought us here." It is prohibited to ask, "What does your husband do?" or "Have you already purchased a home here and settled in?"

You may ask only questions that ascertain pertinent job skills, education, and experience.

APPENDIX **8**

Preliminary Interview Template

Reminder: Inform candidate that this is a preliminary interview. Inform of the position(s) that are open, and other details of application to the district that must be completed.

If the candidate is at a job fair or in a video interview:

	Unacceptable	Acceptable	Target
1. Attire and grooming.	_____	_____	_____
2. Basic interpersonal skills.	_____	_____	_____

General Questions

1. Tell about your most successful teaching experience.

   _____ _____ _____

2. Describe the classroom management in a room where you have worked.

   _____ _____ _____

3. Tell about one lesson that went well and why.

   _____ _____ _____

4. How have you met individual students' needs in your classroom?

   _____ _____ _____

5. How do you know that students are learning?

   _____ _____ _____

6. Add a question about the specific position. We need a first-grade teacher. What are two of the most important curricular standards to meet with this age?

   _____ _____ _____

7. What do you know about our district, and why do you want to
    work here?   _____   _____   _____

Rate the candidate's command of spoken language.

_____   _____   _____

Notes:

APPENDIX **9**

Preschool Interview Questions

Ask the same questions to each candidate, and in the same order.

	Unacceptable	Acceptable	Target
1. Attire and grooming.	_____	_____	_____
2. Basic interpersonal skills.	_____	_____	_____
3. Clear, correct language use.	_____	_____	_____

Questions:

1. Describe a preschool classroom where you have worked and how it was arranged. _____ _____ _____

2. Describe specific procedures and routines in the classroom where you worked. _____ _____ _____

3. Explain a lesson that you have taught that went well, and why it went well. _____ _____ _____

4. What are specific curricular standards that need to be met by three-, four-, and/or five-year-olds?

    _____ _____ _____

5. What are some behavior issues that you have dealt with, and how did you deal with those issues?

    _____ _____ _____

6. How have you managed student behavior with this age group?

    _____ _____ _____

7. Describe an activity that is developmentally appropriate for five-year-olds that will not work with younger students.

    _____ _____ _____

8. How have you communicated with parents about their children?

        _____   _____   _____

9. How have you used parents as volunteers?

        _____   _____   _____

10. How have you differentiated learning for students?

        _____   _____   _____

11. How have you assessed students' work, overall progress, and readiness to move to kindergarten?

        _____   _____   _____

12. Why do you want to work in our preschool?

        _____   _____   _____

Add other questions specific to your school. These may include questions about working with at-risk students, migrant children, English language learners, and so on.

*** What other questions do you have about this position or our school?

Notes:

Elementary School Interview Questions

Ask the same questions to each candidate, and in the same order.

	Unacceptable	Acceptable	Target
1. Attire and grooming.			
2. Basic interpersonal skills.			
3. Clear, correct language use.			

Questions:

1. Describe an elementary classroom where you have worked.

2. Describe the procedures and routines in a classroom that created a well-run atmosphere.

3. Describe a classroom management plan that you have used that worked well.

4. Explain your experience teaching to the Common Core State Standards with this age group.

5. Describe a lesson built on a standard and how you planned and implemented that lesson.

6. Characterize your work with the teaching of reading.

7. Outline how you have integrated subjects.

8. Explain a lesson that students really enjoyed and why they enjoyed it.

9. How have you differentiated your instruction to meet students' needs?   _____ _____ _____

10. How have you used technology in your teaching?

    _____ _____ _____

11. How have you assessed students' work?

    _____ _____ _____

12. How have you determined that students are ready for the next grade level?   _____ _____ _____

Give an example of how you have communicated with parents.

    _____ _____ _____

Characterize your work with other teachers and/or administrators.

    _____ _____ _____

What is your interest in teaching in our school?

    _____ _____ _____

Add other questions specific to your school. These may include questions about working with at-risk students, migrant children, English language learners, and so on.

*** What other questions do you have about this position or our school?

Notes:

APPENDIX **11**

Middle School Questions

Ask the same questions to each candidate, and in the same order.

	Unacceptable	Acceptable	Target
1. Attire and grooming.	_____	_____	_____
2. Basic interpersonal skills.	_____	_____	_____
3. Clear, correct language use.	_____	_____	_____

Questions:

1. Describe a middle school classroom where you have worked (grade, subject, student population).

    _____ _____ _____

2. Describe the classroom management plan in a room where you have worked.   _____ _____ _____

3. Tell about your experiences with team teaching or team planning.   _____ _____ _____

4. Describe a lesson that you taught that was successful and why it was successful.   _____ _____ _____

5. Tell about your experience developing lessons to the Common Core State Standards or other standards.

    _____ _____ _____

6. How have you assessed student learning in a variety of ways?

    _____ _____ _____

7. How have you integrated reading strategies into your subject?

    _____ _____ _____

8. How have you differentiated instruction to meet the needs of students?   _____ _____ _____

9. Describe the maturity levels of middle school students.

    _____   _____   _____

10. What have you done to help middle school students get or stay motivated on academics?   _____   _____   _____

11. How have you determined that students are ready for the next grade level?   _____   _____   _____

12. Give an example of how you have communicated with parents.

    _____   _____   _____

13. Characterize your work with other teachers and/or administrators.

    _____   _____   _____

14. What is your interest in teaching in our school?

    _____   _____   _____

Add other questions specific to your school. These may include questions about working with at-risk students, migrant children, English language learners, and so on.

Ask the candidate:

*** What other questions do you have about this position or our school?

Notes:

APPENDIX **12**

General High School Interview Questions

Ask the same questions to each candidate, and in the same order.

	Unacceptable	Acceptable	Target
1. Attire and grooming.	_____	_____	_____
2. Basic interpersonal skills.	_____	_____	_____
3. Clear, correct language use.	_____	_____	_____

Questions:

1. Describe a high school classroom where you have worked (grade, subject, student population).

   _____ _____ _____

2. Explain the basic procedures and routines in a classroom where you have worked. _____ _____ _____

3. Describe a classroom management plan (including rules and consequences) you have used and why it worked with teenagers.

   _____ _____ _____

4. Describe a lesson that you taught that was successful and why it was successful. _____ _____ _____

5. Tell about your experience developing lessons to the Common Core State Standards or other standards.

   _____ _____ _____

6. How have you used technology in your teaching?

   _____ _____ _____

7. How have you assessed student learning in a variety of ways?

   _____ _____ _____

8. How have you differentiated instruction to meet the needs of students? _____ _____ _____

9. How have you motivated students to graduate?

_____ _____ _____

10. Give an example of how you have communicated with parents.

_____ _____ _____

11. Characterize your work with other teachers and/or administrators.

_____ _____ _____

12. What is your interest in teaching at our school?

_____ _____ _____

Add other questions specific to the discipline and your school (see Appendices 13–18 for sample questions). You may include questions about working with Advanced Placement courses, at-risk students, migrant children, and English language learners.

Ask the candidate:

*** What other questions do you have about this position or our school?

Notes:

APPENDIX **13**

Subject Matter–Specific Questions

Choose from these questions to add to the general template for a grade level.

English/Language Arts

1. What strategies or methods have you used to improve student writing?

2. Describe a rubric or criteria sheet for evaluating a student's writing.

3. How have you prepared students for the standardized tests in English, reading, or language arts?

4. How have your past students scored on standardized tests?

5. Describe your work with developing lessons based on the Common Core State Standards.

6. How have you chosen the books that your students read?

7. Characterize your approach to the teaching of grammar, phonics, or other topics.

Mathematics

1. Characterize a typical math lesson that you have taught.

2. How much time during a typical lesson do you spend guiding students' practice and providing feedback?

3. What is a hot topic in math for this grade level, and how have you addressed this topic in your classes?

4. What are some of the most important topics to cover with this grade level in math?

5. What have you done to ensure that students do their work?

Science

1. Describe how you have used labs in past science classes that you have taught.

2. How have you used technology in past classes that you have taught?

3. Give an example of a hot topic in your field of science and how you have taught or dealt with that topic (e.g., biology and evolution).

4. How have you encouraged and motivated students to learn science?

5. What are some common student complaints about science, and how have you dealt with them?

History/Social Studies/Government

1. When your class is required, how do you interest students in it?

2. Describe a typical lesson, explaining how you have used group work or other activities.

3. How do you stay current in your field?

4. How have you helped students improve their reading and writing skills in your class?

5. Which curricular topics are important "big" topics in your class?

Foreign Languages

1. During what percentage of a typical lesson do you speak and use only the target language (the foreign language being taught)? Why?

2. Characterize your teaching of grammar.

3. How have you incorporated culture into your lessons?

4. How do you keep your command of the language current?

5. There is much debate about how to teach a foreign language. Describe your overall approach to teaching a language.

6. How do you help parents assist their child in learning a language?

7. How have you used technology in the foreign language classroom?

APPENDIX **14**

Health and Physical Education Interview Questions

Ask the same questions to each candidate, and in the same order.

	Unacceptable	Acceptable	Target
1. Attire and grooming.	_____	_____	_____
2. Basic interpersonal skills.	_____	_____	_____
3. Clear, correct language use.	_____	_____	_____

Questions:

1. Tell about your specific experience teaching PE.

   _____   _____   _____

2. Tell about your specific experience teaching health.

   _____   _____   _____

3. Many students do not want to participate in PE. How have you motivated students to do so?

   _____   _____   _____

4. How have you planned lessons? What has guided your lesson planning?   _____   _____   _____

5. Describe your classroom management for PE classes. What consequences have worked well with the students you have taught?

   _____   _____   _____

6. Childhood obesity is a huge issue. How have you worked with overweight students to encourage and support a healthy lifestyle?

   _____   _____   _____

7. How do you assess students and assign grades in PE courses?

_____ _____ _____

8. How have you differentiated instruction or changed the environment to meet the special needs of students in PE?

_____ _____ _____

9. How have you motivated students to graduate?

_____ _____ _____

10. Give an example of how you have communicated with parents.

_____ _____ _____

11. Characterize your work with other teachers and/or administrators.

_____ _____ _____

12. What is your interest in teaching at our school?

_____ _____ _____

Add other questions specific to your school's student population.

Ask the candidate:

*** What other questions do you have about this position or our school?

Notes:

APPENDIX **15**

Art Interview Questions

Ask the same questions to each candidate, and in the same order.

	Unacceptable	Acceptable	Target
1. Attire and grooming.	_____	_____	_____
2. Basic interpersonal skills.	_____	_____	_____
3. Clear, correct language use.	_____	_____	_____

Questions:

1. Describe how you have done long-term planning.

2. Characterize the types of artwork that students have done in your past classes.

3. Describe a typical lesson that you have taught and why it went well.

4. Art classrooms have special arrangements. Describe a well-organized classroom in which you have worked.

5. What is a good classroom management plan for an art classroom?

6. Since art is not assessed on standardized tests, how have you assessed student work and assigned grades?

7. How have you motivated students to work in art?

8. How have you accommodated students with special needs in an art classroom?

9. Give an example of how you have communicated with parents.

_____   _____   _____

10. Characterize your work with other teachers and/or administrators.

.   _____   _____   _____

11. What is your interest in teaching at our school?

_____   _____   _____

Add other questions specific to your school.

Ask the candidate:

*** What other questions do you have about this position or our school?

Notes:

APPENDIX 16

Music Interview Questions

Ask the same questions to each candidate, and in the same order.

	Unacceptable	Acceptable	Target
1. Attire and grooming.	_____	_____	_____
2. Basic interpersonal skills.	_____	_____	_____
3. Clear, correct language use.	_____	_____	_____

Questions:

1. Describe your experience with marching band, concert band, chorus, or general music classes (choose appropriate ones).

   _____   _____   _____

2. Describe a typical class that went well and tell why it went well.

   _____   _____   _____

3. Band and chorus rooms have special arrangements. Describe a well-organized room where you have worked.

   _____   _____   _____

4. What constitutes a good classroom management plan for band/chorus?

   _____   _____   _____

5. Have you taken students off school grounds for performances, and if so, what were the special rules for those trips?

   _____   _____   _____

6. How have you worked with parent groups and/or been involved in fund-raising for music?

   _____   _____   _____

7. How have you accommodated students with special needs in music programs? _____ _____ _____

8. How have you assessed students and assigned grades? Why is this important? _____ _____ _____

9. Characterize your work with other teachers and/or administrators.

_____ _____ _____

10. What is your interest in teaching at our school?

_____ _____ _____

Add other questions specific to your school (e.g., requirements to take the band or chorus to events and competitions, the need to raise funds to keep these programs).

Ask the candidate:

*** What other questions do you have about this position or our school?

Notes:

APPENDIX **17**

Special Education Interview Questions

Ask the same questions to each candidate, and in the same order.

	Unacceptable	Acceptable	Target
1. Attire and grooming.	_____	_____	_____
2. Basic interpersonal skills.	_____	_____	_____
3. Clear, correct language use.	_____	_____	_____

Questions:

1. Describe the classroom(s) where you have worked and the type of supports you provided students.

   _____   _____   _____

2. Tell about your work with (fill in the special student population here, such as autism, ADD, or another special population).

   _____   _____   _____

3. Characterize your work with total inclusion, mainstreaming, or pull-out programs.   _____   _____   _____

4. Describe a lesson that was successful and why it was successful.

   _____   _____   _____

5. How have you used technology to support student learning?

   _____   _____   _____

6. Outline your work with one student's IEP.

   _____   _____   _____

7. Describe your work with RTI (response to intervention).

   _____   _____   _____

8. Discuss your work collaborating with other teachers.

　　　　＿＿＿＿＿＿　＿＿＿＿＿＿　＿＿＿＿＿＿

9. Describe a positive experience communicating with parents or guardians regarding their child.

　　　　＿＿＿＿＿＿　＿＿＿＿＿＿　＿＿＿＿＿＿

10. Describe assessments that you have used.

　　　　＿＿＿＿＿＿　＿＿＿＿＿＿　＿＿＿＿＿＿

11. What is your interest in teaching at our school?

　　　　＿＿＿＿＿＿　＿＿＿＿＿＿　＿＿＿＿＿＿

Add other questions specific to the discipline and your school (see Appendices 9–16 and 18 for sample questions). You may include questions about working with Advanced Placement courses, at-risk students, migrant children, or English language learners.

Ask the candidate:

*** What other questions do you have about this position or our school?

Notes:

APPENDIX **18**

ESOL/ESL Interview Questions

Ask the same questions to each candidate, and in the same order.

	Unacceptable	Acceptable	Target
1. Attire and grooming.	_____	_____	_____
2. Basic interpersonal skills.	_____	_____	_____
3. Clear, correct language use.	_____	_____	_____

Questions:

(Note that ESOL and ESL are used differently for different programs and the names vary by region of the country. In these questions, English for Speakers of Other Languages [ESOL] was chosen, but English as a Second Language may be easily substituted.)

1. Describe the classroom settings where you have worked with ESOL students.   _____ _____ _____

2. Characterize your approaches to teaching ESOL.

   _____ _____ _____

3. Explain methods of teaching that have worked well in your past teaching.   _____ _____ _____

4. Describe a classroom management plan that you have used.

   _____ _____ _____

5. Describe a lesson that went well and why it went well.

   _____ _____ _____

6. How have you used technology in your teaching?

   _____ _____ _____

7. How have you assessed student learning in a variety of ways?

   _____ _____ _____

8. How have you differentiated instruction to meet the needs of students? _____ _____ _____

9. Give an example of how you have communicated with parents or guardians. _____ _____ _____

10. Characterize your work with other teachers and/or administrators.

_____ _____ _____

11. What is your interest in teaching at our school?

_____ _____ _____

Add other questions specific to the discipline and your school. Questions may include knowledge of the culture of the immigrant groups in your district.

Ask the candidate:

*** What other questions do you have about this position or our school?

Notes:

APPENDIX **19**

New Teacher Orientation and Induction Workshops

1. Make the orientation very welcoming, with snacks, a luncheon, a gift bag, and door prizes.

2. An introduction can be a usable activity. Have new teachers introduce themselves as they will on the first day with students.

3. Don't read long handouts or the faculty handbook to attendees. Ask a question and have participants find the answer in their materials.

4. Use activities where teachers are paired for discussion.

5. Use small groups for discussion and role-plays.

6. Have at least one "make it and take it" activity, such as making a poster of the classroom management plan.

7. New teachers should learn the guidelines for the mentoring program and then meet their mentors before school starts.

8. Allow at least one half day for new teachers to work in their rooms with their mentors. Provide guidelines for this time, including making a seating arrangement, making a seating chart, and planning routines and procedures.

9. Provide the dates, times, and agenda for the monthly induction seminars that will follow throughout the year.

10. The monthly seminar topics should include parent communication, grading, classroom management, working with special education students, differentiation, time and stress management, standardized test preparation, and finishing the school year.

11. Evaluate the orientation and seminars.

APPENDIX **20**

Ten Steps for an Effective Mentoring Program

1. Plan a budget and guidelines for the program. Inform/get input from experienced teachers, district administrators, and the school board. Consider the confidentiality of the program in the guidelines (e.g., mentors serving as supporters only, not as evaluators).

2. Appoint a mentoring director who schedules events and pairs the trained mentors with their new teachers.

3. Work with the local teachers' association/union to solicit mentors (as volunteers or for a stipend).

4. Train the mentors in collegial supervision, tenets of adult learning, hot topics in the district, and the roles and responsibilities of serving as a mentor.

5. Schedule a luncheon during the new teacher orientation for mentors and their new teachers to meet.

6. Allow time for the pairs to work together in the new teacher's classroom before the school year begins.

7. Plan time for the pairs to work together throughout the year.

8. Have follow-up training for mentors to share about their work at least once during the year. New teachers will share during their scheduled induction seminars throughout the year.

9. Document the work of the mentoring program. Consider research about retention or student achievement.

10. Have both mentors and new teachers evaluate the work of the program. This includes an evaluation of the mentor by the new teacher.

References

American Association for Employment in Education. (2013). *Job search handbook for educators.* Columbus, OH: Author.

Barley, Z. A. (2009). Preparing teachers for rural appointments: Lessons from the mid-continent. *The Rural Educator, 30*(3), 10–15.

Clement, M. C. (2000). *Building the best faculty: Strategies for hiring and supporting new teachers.* Lanham, MD: Scarecrow Press.

Clement, M. C. (2006). Technology and hiring. *American School Board Journal, 193*(7), 24–26.

Clement, M. C. (2008). *Recruiting and hiring new teachers: A behavior-based approach.* Alexandria, VA: Educational Research Service.

Clement, M. C. (2013). Hiring good colleagues: What you need to know about interviewing new teachers. *The Clearing House, 86,* 99–102.

Clement, M. C., & Wilkins, E. A. (2011). *The induction connection.* Indianapolis, IN: Kappa Delta Pi.

Deems, R. S. (1994). *Interviewing: More than a gut feeling.* West Des Moines, IA: American Media.

Donaldson, M. L. (2011). Principals' approaches to hiring, assigning, evaluating, and developing teachers. *Education Digest, 76*(9), 27–32.

Fitzwater, T. L. (2000). *Behavior-based interviewing: Selecting the right person for the job.* Boston, MA: Thomson.

Ingersoll, R. M., Merrill, L., & May, H. (2012). Retaining teachers: How preparation matters. *Educational Leadership, 69*(8), 30–34.

Ingersoll, R. M., & Smith, R. M. (2003). The wrong solution to the teacher shortage. *Educational Leadership, 60*(8), 30–33.

Janz, T., Hellervik, L., & Gilmore, D. C. (1986). *Behavior description interviewing: New, accurate, cost effective.* Upper Saddle River, NJ: Prentice-Hall.

Kersten, T. (2008). Teacher hiring practices: Illinois principals' perspectives. *Educational Forum, 72,* 355–368.

Liu, E., & Johnson, S. M. (2006). New teachers' experiences of hiring: Late, rushed, and information-poor. *Educational Administration Quarterly, 42,* 324–360.

Marzano, R. J. (2010). Developing expert teachers. In R. J. Marzano (Ed.), *On excellence in teaching* (pp. 213–245). Bloomington, IN: Solution Tree.

O'Donovan, E. (2012). Finding the perfect fit. *District Administration, 48*(1), 23–27.

Rose, D. S., English, A., & Finney, T. G. (2014). *Hire better teachers now.* Cambridge, MA: Harvard Education Press.

Sackett, J. (June 11, 2014). 4 ways technology can improve the hiring process. *eSchool News.* Retrieved from http://www.eschoolnews.com/2014/06/11/technology-hiring-process-241/

Sawchuk, S. (2011, June 8). Districts more strategic about hiring teachers. *Education Week, 30*(33), 1, 11.

Shuls, J., & Maranto, R. (2014). Show them the mission: A comparison of teacher recruitment incentives in high need communities. *Social Science Quarterly, 95*, 239–252.

Stronge, J. H. (2002). *Qualities of effective teachers.* Alexandria, VA: Association for Supervision and Curriculum Development.

Stronge, J. H., & Hindman, J. L. (2006). *The teacher quality index: A protocol for teacher selection.* Alexandria, VA: Association for Supervision and Curriculum Development.

Stronge, J. H., Tucker, P. D., & Hindman, J. L. (2004). *Handbook for qualities of effective teachers.* Alexandria, VA: Association for Supervision and Curriculum Development.

Tooms, A., & Crowe, A. (2004). Hiring good teachers: The interview process: The small nuances of how you and your school are perceived in the interview process can make the difference in attracting high-quality teachers. *Principal, 84*(2), 50–53.

Wasicsko, M. M. (2004). The 20-minute hiring assessment: How to ensure you're hiring the best by gauging educator dispositions. *School Administrator, 61*(9), 40.

Index

A
Advertising strategies
  ad content, 12–13
  job advertisements, 74
  key characteristics, 13
  online sources, 11–12
  recruitment guidelines,
    14, 14 (figure)
American Association for Employment
  in Education (AAEE), 2
Announcements, decision, 61–64
Answer evaluation guidelines,
  34–40, 36 (figure)
Applications, job, 24–25
AppliTrack, 11
Art interview questions, 97–98

B
Barley, Z. A., 9
Behavior-based interviews (BBIs),
  29–33, 31 (figure), 33 (figure)
  see also On-site interviews
Best practices strategies,
  3–4, 4 (figure)

C
Calendar, hiring, 6–8, 8 (figure)
Camp, S. L., 15, 40, 52, 59, 67
Candidate applications and supporting
  paperwork
  art interview questions, 97–98
  assessment guidelines, 26 (figure)
  cover letters, 21–23, 81
  district applications, 24–25
  elementary school interview
    questions, 87–88

ESOL/ESL interview
  questions, 103–104
health and physical education
  interview questions, 95–96
high school interview
  questions, 91–92
letters of recommendation, 22–23
middle school interview
  questions, 89–90
model lesson observation and
  evaluation, 53–55
music interview questions, 99–100
personal qualities, 57–58
portfolios, 26–27, 55–56
preschool interview
  questions, 85–86
resumes, 23–24, 81
sorting criteria, 20–21
special education interview
  questions, 101–102
subject matter-specific interview
  questions, 93–94
  see also Interviews
Canter, Lee, 42, 43 (figure)
Clement, M. C., 6, 9, 11, 16,
  20, 68, 71
Cover letters, 21–23, 81
Crowe, A., 5

D
Decision-making process
  data-informed decisions, 60–61
  decision announcements, 61–64
  district policies, 59–60
  legal issues, 63–64
  nonhire notifications, 62–63

Deems, R. S., 29
Disagreement, 61
Disposition assessments, 2
District applications, 24–25
District hiring policies, 15–16
District job fairs, 46–48
Donaldson, M. L., 1, 3

E
edTPA online portfolio assessment, 55
Effective teachers, 1–2
Elementary school interview
    questions, 87–88
Employment eligibility, 34
English, A., 1, 5, 17, 35, 45, 47–48
English as a Second Language (ESL)
    interview questions, 103–104
English for Speakers of Other
    Languages (ESOL) interview
    questions, 103–104
English language-specific interview
    questions, 93
Evaluation forms, 36–37, 60–61

F
Facebook, 27, 28
Faculty search committees, 16
Final decisions
    see Decision-making process
Finney, T. G., 1, 5, 17, 35, 45, 47–48
Fitzwater, T. L., 29
Foreign language-specific interview
    questions, 94

G
Gilmore, D. C., 29
Google, 27
Government-specific interview
    questions, 94
Group interviews, 47–48
Gwinnett County Public School
    District, Georgia, 52

H
Hand-written signatures, 23
Health and physical education
    interview questions, 95–96

Hellervik, L., 29
High-needs subject areas, 9, 62
High school interview questions,
    91–92
Hindman, J. L., 1, 2
Hiring process
    district policies, 15–16
    hiring calendar, 6–8, 8 (figure)
    hiring philosophy, 6
    key hiring points, 65–66
    legal issues, 63–64
    new hire orientation and training,
        62, 66–70, 68 (figure), 105
    new hire survey, 73
    non-traditional practices, 17 (figure)
    planning strategies, 5
    "start with the end in mind"
        approach, 44
    training guidelines, 77–80
    use of teachers, 16–19, 46,
        66, 75–77
    see also Interviews; Recruiting
        strategies
History-specific interview
    questions, 94

I
Illegal questions
    see Prohibited questions
Implied questions, 34
Inappropriate questions
    see Prohibited questions
Induction programs,
    66–70, 68 (figure), 105
Ingersoll, R. M., 2
INTASC (Interstate Teacher
    Assessment and Support
    Consortium), 26
Interviews
    answer evaluation guidelines,
        34–40, 36 (figure)
    art questions, 97–98
    behavior-based interviews (BBIs),
        29–33, 31 (figure), 33 (figure)
    elementary school teachers, 87–88
    ESOL/ESL questions, 103–104
    group interviews, 47–48

health and physical education
      questions, 95–96
high school teachers, 91–92
middle school teachers, 89–90
music questions, 99–100
on-site interviews, 50–58
preliminary interviews,
      45–49, 83–84
preschool teachers, 85–86
rubrics, 40–44, 41 (figure),
      42 (figure), 43 (figure)
special education questions,
      101–102
"start with the end in mind"
      approach, 44
subject matter-specific questions,
      93–94
telephone interviews, 48–49
see also Prohibited questions

J
Janz, T., 29
Job advertisements, 74
Job applications, 24–25
Job descriptions, 12–13, 14
Job fairs, 45–48
Job market, 2–3
Job Search Handbook for Educators
      (AAEE), 2
Job websites, 11–12
Johnson, S. M., 5, 10
Jones, Fred, 42, 43 (figure)

K
Kersten, T., 1

L
Language arts-specific interview
      questions, 93
Lawsuits, 19
Legal issues, 18–19, 63–64
Legible signatures, 22–23
Letters of recommendation, 22–23
LinkedIn, 11, 27
"Listen fors", 34–35
Liu, E., 5, 10
Local teacher recruitment, 10–11

M
Maranto, R., 9
Marzano, R. J., 1
Mathematics-specific interview
      questions, 93
May, H., 2
McTighe, Jay, 44
Mentoring programs, 68 (figure),
      70–71, 106
Merrill, L., 2
Middle school interview
      questions, 89–90
Model lesson observation and
      evaluation, 53–55
Music interview
      questions, 99–100

N
National online teacher recruitment
      websites, 12
Negotiations
      see Decision-making process
New hire orientation and training,
      62, 66–70, 68 (figure), 105
New hire survey, 73
Nonhire notifications, 62–63
Note-taking, 51

O
O'Donovan, E., 10, 15
Online job applications, 27–28
Online preliminary interviews, 48–49
Online teacher recruitment, 11–12
On-site interviews
      candidate model lesson
            observation and
            evaluation, 53–55
      key characteristics, 56–57
      personal qualities evaluations,
            57–58
      planning guidelines, 51–53
      portfolio assessments, 55–56
      questioning strategies, 50–51
On-site job fairs, 46–48
Orientation, 67–68, 68 (figure)
Oversharing, 57
Oversupply, teacher, 2–3

P

PAR (problem, action, result),
    35, 36 (figure)
Pearson Education, Inc., 55
Philosophy, hiring, 6
Physical education interview
    questions, 95–96
Portfolios, 26–27, 55–56
Potential lawsuits, 19
Preliminary interviews, 45–49, 83–84
Preschool interview questions, 85–86
Professional associations, 11, 12
Professional development,
    16, 68 (figure)
Prohibited questions
    hiring process, 17 (figure)
    interviewing guidelines,
        33–34, 52, 66, 77, 82
    oversharing, 57
    potential lawsuits, 19
    telephone interviews, 48
    training topics, 18, 77
Provisional certification, 62

R

Recommendation, letters of, 22–23
Recruiting strategies
    advertising guidelines,
        11–14, 14 (figure)
    high-needs subject areas, 9, 62
    job fairs, 45–48
    potential sources, 10–11
Red flags, 24, 48–49, 57
Resumes, 23–24, 81
Retention, 2
Role-play scenarios, 78–80
Rose, D. S., 1, 5, 17, 35, 45, 47–48
Rubrics, 40–44, 41 (figure),
    42 (figure), 43 (figure), 61

S

Sackett, J., 11, 28
Sawchuk, S., 3
Science-specific interview
    questions, 94
Search engines, 27–28
Selection protocols, 2

Shortages, teacher, 2–3
Shuls, J., 9
Signatures, 22–23
Skype, 48
Small talk, 34
Smith, R. M., 2
Social media, 27–28
Social studies-specific interview
    questions, 94
Special education interview
    questions, 101–102
Staff training, 19
STAR (situation, task, action, result),
    35, 36 (figure)
"Start with the end in mind"
    approach, 44
Stronge, J. H., 1
Structured interviews, 40
Subject matter-specific interview
    questions, 93–94
Supportive evaluation,
    68, 68 (figure), 71
Support staff
    application sorting, 20–21
    training guidelines, 19, 77
Surpluses, teacher, 2–3
Surveys, new hire, 73

T

Teachers
    art interview questions, 97–98
    elementary school interview
        questions, 87–88
    ESOL/ESL interview questions,
        103–104
    health and physical education
        interview questions, 95–96
    high school interview
        questions, 91–92
    middle school interview
        questions, 89–90
    music interview questions, 99–100
    new hire orientation and
        training, 62, 66–70,
        68 (figure), 105
    as participants in hiring process,
        16–19, 46, 66, 75–77

preschool interview
    questions, 85–86
special education interview
    questions, 101–102
subject matter-specific interview
    questions, 93–94
surpluses and shortages, 2–3
Telephone interviews, 48–49
Templates
    cover letters and resumes, 81
    preliminary interviews, 83–84
    teacher participants, 75–76
Time management, 19
Tooms, A., 5
Training
    answer evaluations, 34–40
    behavior-based interviews (BBIs),
        30–33, 31 (figure), 33 (figure)
    discussion questions, 78–80
    group interviews, 47–48
    mentors, 68 (figure), 70–71, 106
    new hires, 62, 66–70,
        68 (figure), 105
    on-site observations, 53–54
    planning guidelines, 7

resume evaluations, 23–24
role-play scenarios, 78–80
support staff, 19, 77
teacher participants, 18–19, 46,
    66, 75–77
training topics, 18
see also Interviews; Prohibited
    questions
Tucker, P. D., 1

V
Viewyou.com, 11

W
Wasicsko, M. M., 2
Websites
    candidate applications, 27–28
    recruitment strategies, 11–12
Wiggins, Grant, 44
Wilkins, E. A., 68, 71
Wong, Harry, 42, 43 (figure)

Y
Yearlong hiring plan,
    6–8, 8 (figure)

A SAGE Company

Corwin is committed to improving education for all learners by publishing books and other professional development resources for those serving the field of PreK–12 education. By providing practical, hands-on materials, Corwin continues to carry out the promise of its motto: **"Helping Educators Do Their Work Better."**